Living According
to God's Will

T0096563

Living According to God's Will

by Metropolitan Philaret of New York

HOLY TRINITY PUBLICATIONS
The Printshop of St Job of Pochaev
Holy Trinity Monastery
Jordanville, New York

2021

Printed with the blessing of His Eminence,
Metropolitan Hilarion First Hierarch
of the Russian Orthodox Church Outside of Russia

PRINTSHOP OF
SAINT JOB OF POCHAEV

An imprint of

HOLY TRINITY PUBLICATIONS
Holy Trinity Monastery
Jordanville, New York 13361-0036
www.holytrinitypublications.com

ISBN: 978-0-88465-443-8 (paperback)
ISBN: 978-0-88465-448-3 (ePub)
ISBN: 978-0-88465-449-0 (Mobipocket)

Library of Congress Control Number: 2020949549

Cover Image: Photo from pexels.com; Philip Ackermann,
Photographer.

"And he shall be like a tree planted by the water-side, that will bring forth his fruit in due season; his leaf also shall not fall, and all whatsoever he doeth, it shall prosper."

Psalm 1:3

Contents

Foreword

The Lord is constantly calling us to repentance: to reorient the substance of our day-to-day existence toward the attainment of the eternal life He has opened up for us. In this succinct but deeply profound work, where each word is measured, Metropolitan Philaret of blessed memory sets before us the steps on our path to the heavenly kingdom.

It is too often the case that we are ignorant of theology or of an Orthodox understanding of how we should live in a way that is pleasing to God: Such an understanding as is offered in this brief work will open a way to our own purpose and fulfilment in life being found and more fully realized.

In this edition we have augmented the Metropolitan's original text with a series of questions at the end of each of the twenty-nine short chapters. It is our hope that these will further encourage the reader to dwell on what has been said and to understand and follow the wisdom that is contained in them. They also serve to make this book particularly suitable for use by priests, clergy, and other catechists in using this book as a primary text both for the

instruction of new converts and for that of lifelong Orthodox believers who desire to enter into the practice of their
Faith more fully than ever before.

May we all find in Metropolitan Philaret's words aid
in our own struggle against sin and in returning sanity to
a world that all too often today is completely adrift of any
mooring that is anchored in a clear understanding of the
nature of both God and man.

Holy Trinity Monastery, September 2020

CHAPTER I

Conscience and Moral Responsibility

Of all the creatures on earth, only man has an understanding of morality. Every person is aware that one's actions are either good or bad, kind or evil, morally positive or morally negative (immoral). By these concepts of morality, man differs immeasurably from all animals. Animals behave according to their natural characteristics or else, if they have been trained, in the way they are taught. They have, however, no concept of morality-immorality, and so their behavior cannot be examined from the point of view of moral awareness.

By what means does one distinguish between the morally good and the morally bad? This differentiation is made by means of a special moral law given to man by God. This moral law, this voice of God in man's soul, is felt in the depth of our consciousness: it is called conscience. This conscience is the basis of the morality common to man. A person who does not listen to his conscience, but stifles it and suppresses its voice with falseness and the darkness of stubborn sin, is often called unconscionable. The Word of God refers to such stubborn sinners as people with a "seared" conscience (see 1 Tim 4:2). Their spiritual condition is extremely dangerous and can be ruinous for the soul.

When one listens to the voice of one's conscience, one sees that this conscience speaks in him first of all as a judge—strict and incorruptible, evaluating all one's actions and experiences. Often, it happens that some given action appears advantageous to a person, or has drawn approval from others, but in the depths of the soul this person hears the voice of conscience, "This is not good, this is a sin."

In close connection with this action of judging, the conscience also acts in one's soul as a legislator. All those moral demands that confront a person's soul in all his conscious actions (for example, be just, do not steal) are norms, demands, injunctions of this very conscience. Its voice teaches us how one must and must not behave. Finally, the conscience also acts in man as a rewarder. This happens when we, having acted well, experience peace and calm in the soul or, on the other hand, when we experience reproaches of the conscience after having sinned. These reproaches of the conscience sometimes pass over into terrible pain and torment of soul. They can lead a person to despair or a loss of mental balance if one does not restore peace and calmness in the soul through deep and sincere repentance.

It is self-evident that man bears a moral responsibility only for those actions that he commits fully. Only then can moral imputation be applied to these actions, and then they impute to the person either praise or condemnation.

On the other hand, people who are incapable of recognizing the character of their actions (babies, those deprived of reason, etc.) or those who are forced against their will to commit such actions do not bear responsibility for them. In the (first) epoch of persecution against Christianity, the pagan tormentors often placed incense in the hands of martyrs and then held their hands over the flame burning on their altar. The torturers supposed that the martyrs would jerk their hands back, dropping the incense into the fire. In fact, these confessors of the faith were usually so firm in spirit that they preferred to burn their hands and not drop the incense, but even had they dropped it, who would charge that they had brought sacrifice to the idol?

It is understood that one can never consider drunkards to be unaccountable, since they initiated their drunkenness themselves while in a normal and sober state, knowing full well the consequences of drinking. Therefore, in some countries in northern Europe a person who commits a crime while in a drunken state is punished twice: (1) for being drunk and (2) for committing the crime.

That the moral law must be acknowledged as innate to mankind, that is, fixed in the very nature of man, is indisputable. This is bespoken by the undoubted universality in mankind of a concept of morality. Of course, only the most basic moral requirements are innate—a sort of moral instinct—but not so with revealed and clear moral understandings and concepts. For clear moral understandings and concepts develop in man in part through upbringing and influence from preceding generations, most of all on the basis of religious awareness. Therefore, crude pagans have moral norms lower, coarser, and more malformed than Orthodox Christians, those who know and believe in the True God. It was He who placed the moral law into man's soul, and Who, through this law, guides all of their life and activities.

POINTS OF REFLECTION

1. What distinguishes man from other animals?

2. What is conscience?

3. What is the role of conscience in our life?

4. What is the relationship between morality and conscience?

CHAPTER 2

The Nature of Sin

All Orthodox Christians know from the Holy Scripture and believe that God created man in His own image and likeness. Therefore, in the creation man received a sinless nature. But not even the first man, Adam, remained sinless. He lost his original purity in the first fall into sin in paradise. The poison of this sinfulness contaminated the entire human race, which descended from its forbears who had sinned—just as poison water flows from a poisoned spring. Because of the inclination to sin inherited from our ancestors, such that each person commits one's own personal sins, it is not surprising that Holy Scripture says concerning each of us: "For there is not a righteous man on earth who does good and does not sin" (Eccl 7:20; II Chr 6:36). Only our Lord Jesus Christ is absolutely free from sin. Even the righteous, God's Saints, bore sin within themselves, and although with God's help they struggled with it, they humbly acknowledged themselves to be sinners. So, without exception, all people are sinners, tainted with sin.

Sin is a spiritual leprosy, an illness and an ulcer, which has stricken all of mankind, both in his soul and his body. Sin has damaged all three of the basic abilities and powers of the soul: the mind, the heart, and the will. Man's mind became darkened and inclined toward error. Thus, man constantly errs—in science, in philosophy, and in his practical activity.

What is even more harmed by sin is man's heart—the center of his experience of good and evil, and feelings of sorrow and joy. We see that our heart has been bound in the mire of sin; it has lost the ability to be pure, spiritual, and Christian, to possess truly elevated feelings. Instead of this, it has become inclined toward pleasures of sensuality and earthly attachments. It is tainted with vainglory and sometimes startles one with a complete absence of love and of the desire to do good toward one's neighbor.

What is harmed most of all and fettered by sin, however, is our will as the means for performing and realizing one's intentions. Man proves to be without strength of will particularly when it is necessary to practice true Christian good—even though he might desire this good. The holy apostle Paul speaks of this weakness of will when he says: "For the good that I will to do, I do not do; but the evil I will not to do, that I practice" (Rom 7:19). That is why Christ the Saviour said of man, the sinner, "Whoever commits sin is a slave of sin" (John 8:34), although to the sinner, alas, serving sin often seems to be freedom while struggling to escape its nets appears to be slavery.

How does a sin develop in one's soul? The holy fathers, stragglers of Christian asceticism and piety, knowing the sinful human soul, explain it far better than all the learned psychiatrists. They distinguish the following stages in sin: The first moment in sin is the suggestion, when some temptation becomes identified in a person's conscience—a sinful impression, an unclean thought or some other temptation. If, in this first moment, a person decisively and at once rejects the sin, he does not sin but defeats sin and his soul will experience progress rather than degeneration. It is in the suggestion stage of sin that it is easiest of all to remove it. If the suggestion is not rejected, it passes over first into an ill-defined striving and then into a clear conscious desire of sin. At this point, one already begins to be inclined to sin of a given type. Even at this point, however, without an especially difficult struggle, one can avoid giving in to sin and refrain from sinning. One will be helped by the clear voice of conscience and by God's aid if one will only turn to it.

Suppose now that one has fallen into sin. The reproaches of the conscience sound loudly and clearly, eliciting a revulsion to the sin. The former self-assurance disappears and the man is humbled (compare apostle Peter before and after his denial of Christ, Matt 16:21–22;

26:33; Matt 26:69–75). But even at this point, defeat of sin is not entirely difficult. This is shown by numerous examples, as in the lives of St Peter, the Holy Prophet King David, and other repentant sinners.

It is more difficult to straggle with sin when, through frequent repetition, it becomes a habit in one. After acquiring any kind of habit, the habitual actions are performed by the person very easily, almost unnoticed to himself, spontaneously. Thus, the struggle with sin that has become a habit for a person is very difficult since it is not only difficult to overcome but is even difficult to detect in its approach and process.

An even more dangerous stage of sin is vice. In this condition, sin so rules a person that it fetters his will as if in chains. Here, one is almost powerless to struggle against it. He is a slave to sin even though he may acknowledge its danger and, in lucid intervals, perhaps even hates it with all his soul (such for example are the vices of alcoholism, narcotic addiction, etc.). In this condition, one cannot correct oneself without the special mercy and help from God and one is in need of both the prayer and the spiritual support of others. One must bear in mind that even a seemingly minor sin such as gossiping, love of attire, empty diversions, and so forth can become a vice in man if it possesses him entirely and fills his soul.

The highest stage of sin, in which sin completely enslaves one to itself, is the passion of one or another type of sin. In this condition, man can no longer hate his sin as he can with a vice (and this is the difference between them). Rather he submits to sin in all his experiences, actions, and moods, as did Judas Iscariot. At this stage, one literally and directly lets Satan into his heart (as it is said of Judas in the Gospel; see John 13:27; Luke 22:3), and in this condition, nothing will help him except the Grace-filled prayers and rites of the Church.

There is yet another special, most terrible, and destructive type of sin. This is mortal sin. Even the prayers of the Church cannot help one who is found in this condition. The apostle John the Theologian speaks of this directly when he entreats us to pray for a brother that has sinned but points out the uselessness of prayer for mortal sin (1 Jn 5:16).

The Lord Jesus Christ Himself says that this sin—the blasphemy of the Holy Spirit—is not forgiven and will not be forgiven either in this age or in the future (Matt 12:31–32). He pronounced these terrible words against the Pharisees who, though they clearly saw that he worked everything according to the will of God and by God's power, nevertheless distorted the truth, blasphemously maintaining that He acted through the power of an evil, unclean spirit. They perished in their own blasphemy and their example is instructive and terrible for all those who would commit mortal sin—by an obdurate and conscious opposition to the undoubted Truth—and thereby blaspheme the Spirit of Truth, God's Holy Spirit.

We must note that even blasphemy against the Lord Jesus Christ can be forgiven man (according to His own words) since it can be committed in ignorance or temporary blindness. Blasphemy against the Holy Spirit can be forgiven, says St Athanasius the Great, only if a man ceases from it and becomes repentant. But this, sad to say, usually does not happen, since the very nature of the sin is such that it makes it virtually impossible for a man to return to the truth. One who is blind can regain his sight and love the one who revealed the truth to him, and one who is soiled with vices and passions can be cleansed by repentance and become a confessor of the Truth, but who and what can change a blasphemer who has seen and known the Truth and who has stubbornly rejected it and come to hate it? This horrible condition is similar to the condition of the devil himself who believes in God and trembles but who nevertheless hates Him, blasphemes Him, and opposes Him.

When a temptation to sin appears before a man, it usually comes from three sources: from man's own flesh, from the world, and from Satan.

Concerning man's flesh, there is absolutely no doubt that in many respects it is a den and source of anti-moral predispositions, strivings, and inclinations. The ancestral sin—our grievous common inclination toward sin, an inheritance from the sin of our progenitors and our own personal sinful experiences: all this added up and each (experience) strengthening one another—makes in our flesh a source of temptations, sinful moods, and acts.

More often, though, the source of seduction for us is the world around us, which, according to the apostle St John the Theologian, "lies under the sway of the wicked one" (1 Jn 5:19), and friendship with it, according to another apostle, is enmity with God (James 4:4). The milieu around us seduces us, and the people around us do likewise (especially the willful, conscious seducers and corrupters of youth about whom the Lord said, "But whoever causes one of these little ones who believe in Me to sin, it would be better for him if a millstone were hung around his neck, and he were drowned in the depth of the sea" (Matt 18:6)).

The enticers are also external goods, riches, comforts, immoral dances, dirty literature, shameless attire, etc.—all of this is undoubtedly a fetid source of sin and seduction.

But the main and root source of sin is, of course, the devil, as the apostle John the Theologian says, "He who sins is of the devil, for the devil has sinned from the beginning" (1 Jn 3:8). In struggling with God and His Truth, the devil struggles with people, striving to destroy each of us. He struggles most intensely and with the most malice with the Saints, as we see in the Gospel and in the lives of the Saints. We, the sick and infirm, are specially defended by Christ from those fierce temptations to which God's Saints, strong in spirit, are subjected. Nevertheless, Satan does not ignore us. Acting through the enticements of the world and the flesh, he makes them even stronger and more deceptive, also tempting us by sinful suggestions of all kinds. It is because of this that the apostle Peter compares Satan with a "roaring lion" who walketh about "seeking whom he may devour" (1 Pet 5:8).

POINTS OF REFLECTION

1. What are some of the effects of sin in our life and in society?

2. How should we understand freedom?

3. How does sin take root in our life?

4. What are some of the internal and external triggers that cause us to sin?

CHAPTER 3
Virtue

The complete opposite of sin is virtue. Its rudiments are found in every person, as remnants of that natural good that was placed into the nature of man by his Creator. It is found in a pure and complete form only in Christianity, for Christ the Saviour said: "Without Me ye can do nothing" (John 15:5).

Christianity teaches us that man's earthly life is a time of moral struggle, a time of preparation for the future, eternal life. Consequently, the task of man's earthly life consists of correctly preparing for future eternity. The earthly life is brief and it does not repeat itself, for man lives but once on earth. Therefore, in this earthly life, one must work at virtue if one does not wish to destroy one's soul. For this is precisely what God's truth demands of one on the threshold of eternity.

Each Christian, with God's help, is the shaper of his own earthly life in the sense of its course toward virtue.

In order to be virtuous, however, one must not only do good for others but work on oneself, struggling with his insufficiencies and vices, developing in himself a good, Christian-valued foundation. This work on oneself, this struggle in man's earthly life, is indispensable for every Christian. The Lord Himself said: "The kingdom of heaven suffers violence, and the violent take it by force" (Matt 11:12).

The moral character and features of each person are worked out and formed in such a lifelong struggle. A Christian must, of course, be a Christian before all else, a person with an established, solid moral character and he must strive to build such a character. In other words, he must strive for progress in himself toward moral perfection.

Thus, from a Christian point of view, life is a moral struggle, a path of constant striving toward good and perfection. There can be no pause on this path, according to the law of the spiritual life. A man who stops working on himself will not remain the same as he was, but will inevitably become worse—like a stone that is thrown upward and stops rising, it will not remain suspended in the air but will fall downward.

We already know that our sins generally originate from three sources: from the devil, from the world around us lying in evil, and from our own sinful flesh. And since sin is the main enemy and obstacle of virtue, it is evident that a Christian who is striving toward virtue must, with God's mercy and help, struggle against sin in all its aspects. It is especially needful at this point to recall the Saviour's words to the Apostles in the Garden of Gethsemane: "Watch and pray, lest you enter into temptation" (Matt 26:41). The words are directed not only at the Apostles but to all of us, indicating that the struggle with sinful temptations is possible only for one who is vigilant and who prays, standing on guard for his survival.

POINTS OF REFLECTION

1. Why is sin the opposite of virtue?

2. Can we attain a virtuous life without struggling against sin?

CHAPTER 4

God's Law

The task of man's earthly life is preparing himself for eternal salvation and blessedness. To attain this, a man must live in a holy and pure manner—that is, according to God's will.

How can one recognize this will of God? First of all, one's conscience is called God's voice in the soul of man. If the fall had not darkened the human soul, man would be able unerringly and firmly to direct the path of his life according to the dictates of his conscience, in which the inner moral law is expressed. We know, however, that in a sinful man, not only are the mind, heart, and will damaged, but the conscience is also darkened and its judgment and voice have lost their firm clarity and strength. It is not without reason that some people are called unconscionable.

Therefore, conscience alone, the inner voice, became insufficient for man to live and act according to God's will. The need arose for an external guide, for a Divinely revealed law. Such a law was given by God to people in two aspects: first, the preparatory, the Old Testament law of Moses and then the full and perfect law of the Gospel.

There are two distinguishable parts in Moses' law: the religious-moral part and the national-ceremonial part, which was closely tied with the history and way of life of the Jewish nation. Of course, the second aspect has passed into history for Christians, that is, the national-ceremonial rules and laws. But the religious-moral laws preserve their force in Christianity. Therefore, all the ten commandments in the law of Moses are obligatory for Christians and Christianity has not altered them. On the contrary, Christianity has taught people to understand these commandments, not externally or literally, in the manner of blind, slavish obedience, and external fulfillment, but it has revealed the full spirit and taught the perfect and full understanding and fulfillment of them. For Christians, however, Moses' law has significance only because its central commandments (the ten that deal with love of God and neighbors) are accepted and shown forth by Christianity. We are guided in our life not by this preparatory and temporary law of Moses, but by the perfect and eternal law of Christ. St Basil the Great says, "If one who lights a lamp before himself in broad daylight seems strange, then how much stranger is one who remains in the shadow of the law of the Old Testament when the Gospel is being preached." The main distinction of the New Testament law from that of the Old Testament consists in that the Old Testament law looked at the exterior actions of man, while the New Testament law looks at the heart of man, at his inner motives. Under the Old Testament law, man submitted himself to God as a slave to his master, but under the New Testament, he strives toward submitting to Him as a son submits to a beloved father.

There is a tendency to regard the Old Testament law incorrectly: some see no good in it but only seek out features of coarseness and cruelty. This is a mistaken view. It is necessary to take into consideration the low level of spiritual development at which man then stood thousands of years ago. Under the conditions of the times, with truly coarse and cruel morals, those rules and norms of Moses' law that now seem cruel to us (e.g., "eye for eye, tooth for tooth, hand for hand" [Exod 21:24], and so forth) in reality were not such. They did not, of course, destroy human cruelty and vengeance (only the Gospel could do this), but they did restrain it and establish firm and strict limits upon it. Moreover, it must be remembered that those commandments about love toward God and neighbors, which the Lord indicated as the most important, are taken directly from the law of Moses (Mark 12:29–31). The holy apostle Paul says of this law: "Therefore the law is holy, and the commandment holy and just and good" (Rom 7:12).

POINTS OF REFLECTION

1. What is the primary goal of our earthly life?

2. How does awareness of this goal affect the way we live day by day?

3. From where can we learn what God's will is in any given situation so that we can act in accordance with it?

CHAPTER 5

Freedom of Will

We realize that man bears the responsibility for his actions only when he is free in doing them. But does he have that spiritual freedom, a freedom of the will that is presupposed here? Recently, a teaching has spread, which is called determinism. The followers of this teaching, determinists, do not acknowledge freedom of will in man. They declare that in each separate action, man acts only in accordance with external causes. According to their teaching, in every situation man acts only under the influence of motives and impulses, which do not depend upon him, and usually submits himself to the strongest of these motives. Their scholars say, "It only seems to us that we act freely. This is self-deceit."

The eminent seventeenth-century philosopher Spinoza (1632–1677) defends this opinion. As an example, he spoke of a stone that is thrown. If this stone could think and speak, it too would say that it is flying toward and falling upon the spot that it desires. But in reality, it flies only because someone threw it and it falls under the action and power of gravity.

We will return to this example later, but meanwhile let us note the following. The teaching that is opposite to determinism and that acknowledges man's freedom of will is called indeterminism. This teaching is accepted by Christians. But it is necessary to remember that there are extreme indeterminists, whose teaching has a one-sided, false character. They claim that man's freedom is his full authority to act precisely as he desires. In their understanding, therefore, man's freedom is his complete free will, authority to act upon his every desire or whim (the holy apostle Peter speaks concerning such "freedom": "as free, yet not using liberty as a cloak for vice" (1 Pet 2:16; see also 2 Pet 2:19). This is not freedom, of course: this is an evil use of freedom, a distortion of it. Man does not have absolute, unconditional freedom; only All-Mighty God possesses such exalted creative freedom.

In contrast to such false indeterminism, true indeterminism teaches correctly. Its teaching recognizes that man is undoubtedly under the influence of motives and impulses of the most varied types. Thus, for example, the surrounding milieu, conditions of life, the political situation, one's education, cultural development, and so forth act upon him. All this is reflected in the features of his moral countenance. In this recognition that various external motives and influences act upon man, and sometimes very strongly, the indeterminists are in accord with the determinists. But beyond this, there is a deep separation. While the determinists say that man acts one way or another only under the influences of the strongest of the motives, but does not have freedom, the indeterminists recognize that he is always free to choose any of the motives. This motive does not at all need to be the strongest. Moreover, man can even prefer a motive that, to other people, seems to be clearly disadvantageous and unprofitable. The zeal of the holy martyrs serves as an example of this. To their pagan persecutors, they seemed to be fools consciously destroying themselves. Thus, in the opinion of indeterminists, man's freedom is not an unconditional creative freedom, but a freedom of choice; the freedom of our will decides whether one acts one way or another. Christianity accepts precisely such an understanding of human freedom, agreeing with indeterminism. Applying it to the realm of morals, to the question of the struggle between good and evil, between virtue and sin, Christianity declares that man's freedom is his freedom of choice between good and evil. According to a learned theological definition, "freedom of the will is our capability, independent of anyone and anything, of determining for ourselves concerning good and evil."

Now we can immediately set aside Spinoza's example of the falling stone. We realize that man possesses a free will in the sense of a choice of acting in one way or another. Spinoza considers the actions of the flying stone analogous with man's actions. This comparison could have been made only if the stone had a freedom of choice to fly or not to fly, to fall or not to fall. But a stone, of course, has no such freedom and the given example is altogether unconvincing.

The insolvency of determinism, which negates the freedom of the will, is evident from the following. Firstly, not a single determinist effects his teaching in practical life. And it is clear precisely why. For if one is to look at life from a strictly deterministic point of view, there is no need to punish anyone—neither the thief for thievery nor the murderer for murder, etc.—since they did not act freely but were slaves, unwilling fulfillers of whatever motives commanded them and which influenced them from with-out, an absurd but completely inevitable deduction from determinism. Secondly, proof of the freedom of the will is served by the fact of the experience of the soul, which is called to repentance, an experience personally well known to everyone. What is this feeling of repentance based upon? It is evident that it is based upon the fact that the repentant man returns in thought to the moment of the performance of his wrong action, and weeps over his sin, clearly acknowledging that he could have acted otherwise, could have done not evil, but good. Clearly, such repent-ance could not have had a place if man did not possess free will but was an unwilling slave to external influences. In such a case he would not have answered for his action.

We Christians acknowledge man to be morally free and the guide of his own personal will and actions and responsible for them before God's truth. And such freedom is the greatest gift to man from God, Who seeks from man not a mechanical submission, but a freely given filial obedience of love. The Lord Himself affirmed this freedom, "If anyone desires to come after Me, let him deny himself, and take up his cross, and follow Me" (Matt 16:24). Again, in the Old Testament He said through the prophet: "See, I set before you today life and death, good and evil … choose life, that both you and your seed may live" (Deut 30:15, 19).

POINTS OF REFLECTION

1. Should God hold us to account for our actions?

2. Can we overcome the limitations of our own circumstances when seeking to follow God's will?

CHAPTER 6

The Christian "I"

Living in this world, a Christian is in a constant, lively intercourse with God and with his neighbors. In addition to this, during the course of his whole life, he cares for himself, for his physical well-being, and for the salvation of his soul. His moral obligations, therefore, can be divided into three groups: (1) obligations concerning himself, (2) concerning neighbors, and (3) highest of all, concerning God.

The first, and the most important obligation that man has concerning himself, is the development within oneself of a spiritual character, of our true, Christian "I." The spiritual character of a Christian is not something given to him at first. No, it is something sought for, acquired, and worked out by his personal toils and efforts. Neither the body of a Christian with its capabilities, powers, and strivings, nor his soul itself—as an innate center of his conscious experiences and as a vital principle—is his spiritual personality, the spiritual "I." This spiritual character in an Orthodox Christian is what sharply differs him from every non-Christian. In the Holy Scripture it is not called a soul, but a spirit. This spirit is precisely the center, the concentration of the spiritual life; it strives toward God and the immortal, blessed, eternal life.

We define the task of the entire life of man as the necessity to use the earthly, transitory life for preparation toward the eternal, spiritual life. In this instance, it can be said in other words. The task of the earthly life of man consists of building up and developing, in the course of this life, his spiritual character, his true, living, eternal "I."

One can care about one's "I" in different ways. There are people who are called egotists and who cherish and are concerned very much with their "I." An egoist, however, thinks only of himself and about no one else. In his egoism, he strives to obtain his personal happiness by any useful means—even at the cost of suffering and misfortune for neighbors. In his blindness, he does not realize that, from the true point of view, in the sense of the Christian understanding of life, he only harms himself, his immortal "I."

And here Orthodox Christianity (i.e., the Holy Church), calling upon man to create his spiritual character, directs him in the course of this development, to distinguish good and evil and the truly beneficial from the pretended beneficial and harmful. She (the Holy Church) teaches us that we cannot consider the things given us by God (ability, talents, etc.) to be our "I"; rather we must consider them gifts of God. We must use these gifts (like materials in the construction of a building) for the building of our spirit. For this, we must use all these "talents" given by God, not for ourselves egoistically, but for others. For the laws of Heaven's Truth are contradictory to the laws of earthly gain. According to worldly understandings he who gathers for himself on earth acquires wealth; according to the teaching of God's Heavenly Truth, he who, in the earthly life, gives away and does good acquires (for eternity). In the well-known parable about the indolent steward, the main thought and the key to the correct understanding of it is the principle of contradistinction between the understandings of the earthly egoism and God's truth. In this parable, the Lord specifically called earthly wealth, gathered egoistically for oneself, "unjust wealth," and ordered that it not be used for oneself, but for others, in order that one may be received in the eternal home.

The ideal of Christian perfection is unattainably high. "You shall be perfect, just as your Father in heaven is perfect," Christ the Saviour said (Matt 5:48). Therefore, there can be no end to the work of a man on himself, on his spiritual character. The entire earthly life of a Christian is a constant struggle of moral self-perfection. And, of course, Christian perfection is not given to a man at once, but gradually. To a Christian who, through his inexperience, thought that he could attain holiness at once,

St Seraphim of Sarov said, "Do everything slowly, not suddenly; virtue is not a pear—you cannot eat it at once." Nor did the apostle Paul in all his spiritual height and power consider himself as having reached perfection but said that he was only striving toward such perfection,

> Not that I have already attained, or am already perfected; but I press on, that I may lay hold of that for which Christ Jesus has also laid hold of me. Brethren, I do not count myself to have apprehended; but one thing I do, forgetting those things which are behind and reaching forward to those things which are ahead, press toward the goal for the prize of the upward call of God in Christ Jesus. (Phil 3:12–14).

POINTS OF REFLECTION

1. To whom do we have obligations?

2. How does attaining spiritual perfection contrast with acquiring worldly wealth?

CHAPTER 7

Humility

According to the teachings of our Holy and God-bearing Fathers, the athletes, and lamps of Christian piety, the first of all Christian virtues is humility. Without this virtue, no other virtue can be acquired, and the spiritual perfection of a Christian is unthinkable. Christ the Saviour begins His New Testament precepts of blessedness with the precept of humility: "Blessed are the poor in spirit, for theirs is the kingdom of heaven" (Matt 5:3).

In the usual sense of the word, we consider a person poor who has nothing and must ask others for help. The Christian (whether materially rich or poor) must recognize that he is spiritually poor, that there is no good of his own within him. Everything good in us is from God. From our own selves, we add only evil—self-love, sensual capriciousness, and sinful pride. Each of us must remember this, for it is not in vain that the Holy Scripture says: "God resists the proud, but gives grace to the humble" (1 Pet 5:5).

As we have already said, without humility, no other virtue is possible, for if man does not fulfill virtue in a spirit of humility, he will inevitably fall into God-opposing pride and will fall away from God's mercy.

Together with a true, deep humility, each Christian must have spiritual mourning such as that spoken of in the second precept on blessedness. Who does not know that humility in a person is often shallow and false? There is a good reason for the expression: "some humility is worse than pride." Often it seems that someone is humbling and condemning himself. However, it turns out that this is not a profound, constant frame of mind and experience of the soul, but a superficial, shallow feeling. The Holy Fathers indicated one manner by which the sincerity and depth of humility can be recognized.

Begin to reproach a person to his face, for those very sins and in those very expressions in which he "humbly" judges himself. If his humility is sincere, he will hear out the reproaches without anger and sometimes will thank you for the humbling instruction. If he does not have true humility, he will not endure the reproaches but will become angry, since his pride will rear up on its haunches from the reproaches and accusations.

The Lord says, "Blessed are those who mourn, for they shall be comforted" (Matt 5:4). In other words, blessed are they who not only sorrow over their own imperfection and unworthiness but mourn over it. By mourning we understand, first of all, spiritual mourning—weeping over sins and the resultant loss of God's Kingdom. Moreover, among the ascetics of Christianity, there were many who, filled with love and compassion, wept over other people—over their sins, falls, and sufferings. It is also in keeping with the spirit of the Gospel to count as mourners all those sorrowing and unfortunate people who accept their sorrow in a Christian way: humbly and submissively. They are truly blessed, for they shall be comforted by God, with love. And those who, on the contrary, seek to obtain only pleasure and enjoyment in the earthly life are not at all blessed. Although they consider themselves fortunate, and others consider them as such, according to the spirit of the Gospel teaching, they are most unfortunate people. It is precisely to them that this threatening warning of the Lord is directed: "But woe to you who are rich, for you have received your consolation. Woe to you who are full, for you shall hunger. Woe to you who laugh now, for you shall mourn and weep" (Luke 6: 24–25).

When a man is filled with humility and sorrow for his sins, he cannot make peace with that evil of sin, which so stains both himself and other people. He strives to turn away from his sinful corruption and from the untruth of the surrounding life—to turn to God's truth, to holiness and purity. He seeks this truth of God and its triumph over human untruths and desires it more strongly than one who is hungry desires to eat, or one who is thirsty desires to drink.

The fourth precept, which is bound to the first two, tells us of this: "Blessed are those who hunger and thirst for righteousness, for they shall be filled" (Matt 5:6).

When shall they be filled? In part, here in the earthly life, in which these faithful followers of God's truth already see, at times, the beginnings of its triumph and victory in the actions of God's Providence and in the manifestations of God's justice and omnipotence. But their spiritual hunger and thirst will be satisfied and quenched in full there, in blessed eternity, in the "new heavens," and in the "new earth in which righteousness dwells" (2 Pet 3:13).

POINTS OF REFLECTION

1. What is the underpinning of all virtues?

2. What are the characteristics of genuine, salvific humility?

∽ CHAPTER 8
Conversion of Sinners

We have discussed the subjects of man's free will and examined the first of virtues—humility, spiritual mourning, and striving toward God's Truth. Now, we must speak of the process of the conversion of an erring sinner to the path of righteousness. The parable of the Prodigal Son (Luke 15:11–32) is the best example of this process. This parable tells us of a young son who is annoyed by the careful guardianship of his father. The son senselessly decided to betray his father, and came to him asking for his share of the inheritance. Having received it, he departed into a distant country. It is clear that this senseless son represents each sinner. Man's betrayal of God is usually manifested in this way—one receives everything that God has given one in life, and then ceases to have fervent faith in Him, ceases to think about Him and to love Him, finally, forgetting about His law. Is this not like the life of many contemporary intellectuals? Overlooking what is truly essential, they live in remoteness from God. In that far away land, so deceiving from a distance, the senseless son squandered and wasted his possessions, living dissolutely. Thus it is that the senseless sinner wastes his spiritual and physical strength in the pursuit of sensual enjoyments and in "burning through his life," he departs, in heart and soul, further and further from his Heavenly Father.

The prodigal son, having squandered his possessions, grew so hungry that he took a job as a swineherd (a keeper of animals that, according to Mosaic law, were impure). He would have been glad to eat swine's food, but no one gave him any. Is it not so that a sinner, entangled finally in the nets of sin, hungers spiritually, suffers, and languishes? He tries to fill his spiritual emptiness with a whirlpool of empty pleasures, reveling, and dissipatedness. But all this is "swine's food" which cannot drown the torment of hunger from which his deathless spirit grows weak.

The unfortunate one would perish if it were not for help from God, Who Himself said that He does not desire the death of the ungodly man but that he should be converted and live (see Ezek 33:11). The prodigal son heard the call of God's Grace and he did not push it aside nor reject it, but he accepted it. He accepted it and came to himself as one who is ill comes to himself after a tortuous incubus. There was a saving thought: "How many of my father's hired servants have bread enough and to spare, and I perish with hunger! I will arise," he decides, "and go to my father, and will say to him, 'Father, I have sinned against heaven and before you, and I am no longer worthy to be called your son. Make me like one of your hired servants.'" A firm intention, a decisive resolve—he arose and went to his father.

He went, all penetrated with repentance, burning with the consciousness of his guilt and unworthiness—and with hope of the father's mercy. His way was not easy. But when he was yet far off, his father saw him (it means that the father was waiting and was perhaps looking every day to see if the son was returning). He saw and took pity, and running out, threw his arms around his shoulders and kissed him. The son was about to begin his confession: "Father, I have sinned against heaven and before you, and I am no longer worthy to be called your son." But the father did not allow him to finish. He had already forgiven and forgotten all, and accepted the dissolute and hungry swineherd as a beloved son (see Luke 15:20–24). The Lord said that "there will be more joy in heaven over one sinner who repents than over ninety-nine just persons who need no repentance" (Luke 15:7).

So gradually the process of falling away and conversion to God occurs in one. One is, as it were, lowered and then elevated by steps—at first, betrayal of God, going away from Him to a "distant country." In this alienation from God, there is a complete serving of sin and passions. Finally, there is a full spiritual bankruptcy, a spiritual hunger and darkness—the person has reached the depth of falling. Here, however, according to the words of the apostle Paul, where sin has multiplied, an abundance of Grace appears to instruct man. The sinner accepts the saving, Graceful appeal (or rejects it and perishes—and alas, this happens). He accepts it, and comes to himself, and firmly decides to part with sin and go with repentance to the Heavenly Father. He goes along the path of repentance, and the Father comes out to meet him and accepts him, all forgiven and with as much love as ever.

POINTS OF REFLECTION

1. What causes us to drift away from God and to seek comfort in this temporal life?

2. If we abandon God but then subsequently return to Him, how do we expect Him to react?

∞ CHAPTER 9
Grace and Salvation

Speaking about every truly good Christian activity, the Lord Jesus Christ said, "Without Me you can do nothing" (John 15:5). Therefore, when the matter of salvation is being considered, the Orthodox Christian must remember that the beginning of that truly Christian life, which saves us, comes only from Christ the Saviour and is given to us in the mystery of baptism.

In His conversation with Nikodemus about how one enters into God's Kingdom, our Saviour replied: "Most assuredly, I say to you, unless one is born again, he cannot see the kingdom of God" (John 3:3). Furthermore, He clarified this saying: "Unless one is born of water and the Spirit, he cannot enter the kingdom of God" (John 3:5). Baptism is, therefore, that door through which alone one can enter into the Church of those being saved. For only the one who will have faith and be baptized will be saved (see Mark 16:16).

Baptism washes away the corruption of the ancestral sin, and it washes away the guilt of all sins previously committed by the one being baptized. Nevertheless, the seeds of sin—sinful habits and desires toward sin—remain in one and are overcome by means of lifelong moral struggle (man's efforts in cooperation with God's Grace). For, as we already know, God's Kingdom is acquired by effort, and only those who use effort attain it. Other holy mysteries (sacraments) of the Church—repentance, Holy Communion, anointing, and various prayers and divine services—are moments and means of sanctifying a Christian. According to the measure of his faith, a Christian receives divine Grace in them, which facilitates his salvation. Without this Grace, according to Apostolic teaching, we not only cannot do good, but we cannot even wish to do it (see Phil 2:13).

If, however, the help of God's Grace has such immense significance in the matter of our salvation, then what do our personal efforts mean? Perhaps the entire matter of salvation is done for us by God and we only have to "sit with arms folded" and await God's mercy? In the history of the Church, this question was clearly and decisively settled in the fifth century. A strict and learned monk, Pelagius, began to teach that man is saved by himself, by his own strength, without God's Grace. Developing his idea, he finally reached a point at which, in essence, he began to negate the necessity itself of redemption and salvation in Christ. The eminent teacher Augustine (of Hippo) stepped forth against this teaching and demonstrated the necessity of the Lord's Grace for salvation. While refuting Pelagius, however, Augustine fell into the opposite extreme. According to his teaching, everything in the matter of salvation is done for man by God's Grace, and man has only to accept this salvation with gratitude.

As usual, the truth is between these two extremes. It was expressed by the fifth-century ascetic St John Cassian, whose explanation is called synergism (cooperating). According to this teaching, man is saved only in Christ, and God's Grace is the main acting strength in this salvation. Nevertheless, besides the action of God's Grace for salvation, the personal efforts of man himself are also necessary. Man's personal efforts alone are insufficient for his salvation, but they are necessary, for without them, God's Grace will not begin to work out the matter of his salvation.

Thus, man's salvation is worked out simultaneously through the action of God's saving Grace and through the personal efforts of man himself. According to the profound expression of certain of the Fathers of the Church, God created man without the participation of man himself—but He does not save him without his agreement and desire, for He created him unfettered. Man is free to choose good or evil, salvation or ruin, and God does not impede his freedom, although He constantly summons him to salvation.

POINTS OF REFLECTION

1. Why do we still sin after baptism?

2. How do we work together with God to overcome sin in our life?

CHAPTER 10

Learning and Religion

Psychologists recognize three basic powers or capabilities in man's soul: mind, emotion (heart), and will. Through his mind, man acquires knowledge of the surrounding world and its life, and also of all the conscious experiences of his personal soul. Through his emotions (heart), man responds to the effects and impressions from the external world and from his own experiences. Some of them are pleasant for him and he likes them; others are disagreeable and he does not esteem them. Moreover, one person's concepts of "pleasant" and "disagreeable" do not coincide with those of another. What one person likes is not always liked by another and vice versa (from this fact, we derive the saying, "In matters of taste there can be no dispute"). Finally, man's will is that strength of soul through which he enters into the world and acts in it. Man's moral character depends very strongly upon the character and direction of his will.

Returning to the question of the development in man of his spiritual personality, we must note that in working on his "I," man must develop those capabilities of his soul—mind, heart, and will—correctly and in a Christian way. Man's mind develops most rapidly of the three, primarily through the study of the sciences and through education. It is not correct to think that Christianity considers the so-called worldly sciences or education as unnecessary (or even harmful). The whole history of the Church in the ancient centuries speaks against this erroneous view. It is sufficient just to look at the three great teachers and hierarchs, Sts Basil the Great, Gregory the Theologian, and John Chrysostom. They were among the most highly educated people of their time, having learned well the purely worldly science of their era. The science of that era bore a definite pagan cast, but they were able to master what was necessary and useful in this learning and to discard what was useless and unnecessary. Moreover, we must value learned worldly education now, when past pagan admixtures have disappeared from learning and it strives for a comprehension of pure truth. It is true that even now many scholars erroneously assume that science contradicts religion and they add their anti-religious views to scientific truths. But pure science is not at fault in this and Christianity always greets and blesses serious worldly education in which the thinking powers and capabilities of man are formed and strengthened.

It is self-understood that a Christian, while accepting worldly education, places an even greater significance upon religious education (and upbringing). One must remember that Christianity is not solely and exclusively a sphere of experiences and feelings. No, Christianity is a completely finished cycle, a system of corresponding knowledges, of the most varied data relating not only to the religious, but also to the scientific area. To begin with, how can we Christians not know the life of the Saviour, His miracles, and teaching? How, moreover, can we not know the history of our Holy Church and its divine services, which must be known and understood and, therefore, studied?

The significance of Christianity as an all-sided and finished system of learning is particularly clearly seen in the courses in Christian morality and doctrine (formerly taught in Russian secondary schools). In these, Christianity is seen to be a very rich system of learning, encompassing and explaining to man the whole world, and himself, and showing the true sense and aim of his earthly life.

But this too must be remembered. Having received the learning of a religious education, the fullness of knowledge about God's Truth, man, knowing truth, must serve it and heed its voice. The Lord Himself said, "He who is not with Me is against Me" (Matt 12:30). And in relation to Him and His holy will and law, indifference, coldness, and failure to fulfill this law are disastrous for the soul and make man an enemy of Christ and His Truth. Thus, one must never forget His words: "Why do you call Me 'Lord, Lord,' and not do the things which I say?" (Luke 6:46). Similarly, His apostle says, "For not the hearers of the law are just in the sight of God, but the doers of the law will be justified" (Rom 2:13).

POINTS OF REFLECTION

1. How can we distinguish mind, heart, and will?

2. Is secular education inherently hostile to Christian Faith? If not, why not?

3. In the Middle Ages theology was sometimes referred to as "the Queen of Sciences." What does this mean?

CHAPTER 11

Emotional Development

L et us now turn to the matter of the development of man's heart. Under the category of the heart, we understand the capability of pleasant and disagreeable sensations. These sensations are of different sorts, from the lowest organic sensations up to the highest esthetic moral and religious feelings. The higher feelings are also called emotions. The education of man's heart consists in the development of these emotions in it.

Let us pause on one such emotion—the esthetic feeling. "Esthetic feeling" is the term that signifies the sense of the beautiful, the ability of man to behold and understand, to enjoy and be enthralled by any beauty, by all things beautiful, no matter where or how they appear to us. Such delight in beauty can reach either a turbulent, fiery ecstasy or a quiet, calm, profound feeling. Thus, the esthetic feeling is indissolubly tied with the idea of the beautiful, with the concept of beauty.

"But," one asks, "what is beauty?"

This question may have different answers. The best reply is this: beauty is the full harmony between the content and form of a given idea. The purer, the more salient, and more perfect the form in which this idea is transferred, the more there will be beauty present, the more beautiful the phenomenon will be. Of course, Orthodox Christianity sees the highest beauty in God, in Whom there is the fullness of all beauty and perfection.

Esthetic feeling of one degree or another is inherent in every person but is far from being developed correctly, in full measure, in every case. Its proper development and direction are brought about by uncovering the person's ability to correctly evaluate one or another example or work of art. An aesthetically educated person is able to find features of perfection and beauty in a good picture, composition, or literary work. He can himself understand and appreciate it and can explain to another what, precisely, is beautiful in a given work of art, what its content is, and in what form it is transferred.

Orthodox Christianity knows how to appreciate and love beauty. And we see beauty in Orthodoxy everywhere—in church architecture, in the divine services, in the music of church singing, and in iconography. Moreover, it is notable that beauty in nature was loved and valued by the strictest of our ascetics, who had completely renounced the world. The leading monasteries of Russia were founded in localities distinguished by their beauty.

In this, the bright spirit of Orthodoxy is manifested in its relationship to everything truly beautiful. In the Gospel we see how Christ our Saviour tenderly and lovingly regarded lilies of the field, birds, fig trees, and grapevines. Even in the Old Testament times the Prophet King David, contemplating the beauty and majesty of God's creation, exclaimed, "How great are Thy works, O Lord! In wisdom hast Thou made them all; the earth is filled with Thy handiwork" (Ps 103:24 LXX). In another psalm, he addresses nature as if it were conscious, saying, "Let every thing that hath breath praise the Lord" (Ps 150:6 LXX); "Praise Him, sun and moon; praise Him all ye stars and light" (Ps 148:3).

But, of course, Orthodox Christianity cannot limit its concept of the truly beautiful only to what pleases our sense of beauty by the elegance of its form but must see as truly beautiful all that is morally valuable. True beauty always elevates, ennobles, enlightens man's soul, and sets before it the ideals of truth and good. An Orthodox Christian never acknowledges as beautiful that phenomenon or work of art that, even though it be of perfect execution, does not purify and enlighten man's soul but rather debases and soils it.

POINTS OF REFLECTION

1. What makes someone or something beautiful?

2. What are the characteristics of true beauty?

3. What is the role of beauty on the path to salvation?

CHAPTER 12

Emotional Development in Children and on Christian Hope

The esthetic feeling that we examined in the preceding chapter is but one of the emotions of the human heart. Understandably, many other emotions have a greater significance for the Christian. For example, the elevated feelings of sympathy and antipathy; of familial, filial, and national ties; of mercy, compassion, etc. must be developed in the heart of the Orthodox Christian, if possible, from the very earliest years.

Alas, all too often this does not happen. Unfortunately, in many good Orthodox Christian families, life is arranged in such a way that the parents consciously guard their children from contact with human need, sorrow, heavy difficulties, and trials. Such an excessive protection of children from sober reality brings only negative results. Children who have grown up under greenhouse conditions, separated from life, grow up soft, spoiled, and not well adjusted for life, often thick-skinned egotists, accustomed only to demanding and receiving and not knowing how to yield, to serve, or to be useful to others. Life can break such people cruelly and sometimes punishes them unbearably, often from their early school years. It is necessary, therefore, for those who love their children to temper them. Above all, there must always be one definite Orthodox Christian aim set before both parents and children: that children, while growing and developing physically, must also grow and develop spiritually, and that they become better, kinder, more pious, and more sympathetic.

In order to accomplish this, however, it is necessary to allow children to come into contact with people's needs and wants and to give them the opportunity to help. Then children themselves will strive for goodness and truth, for everything that is pure, good, and bright is especially near to the soul of the unspoiled child.

Those emotions about which we have spoken, including the highest of them, mercy and compassion, are encountered in all people. Speaking now of feelings of a purely Christian kind, we pause on the feeling of Christian hope. Christian hope can be defined as a sincere, vivid remembrance of God, inseparably tied with the assurance of His Fatherly love and help. A man who has such hope always and everywhere feels himself under the Father's protection just as he everywhere and always sees the infinite vault of heaven above him in the physical world. Therefore, an Orthodox Christian having hope in God will never come to despair and will never feel himself hopelessly alone. A situation can seem hopeless only to an unbeliever. A believer, one who hopes in God, knows His nearness to the sorrowing human heart and will find comfort, courage, and help in Him.

Of course, the crown and summit of Christian hope is in the future. We Orthodox Christians know that our Symbol of Faith, in which all the basic truths of Christianity are gathered, ends with the words, "I look for [expect and earnestly long for] the resurrection of the dead; and the life of the age to come. Amen" (The Divine Liturgy of St John Chrysostom).

So a full realization of the bright Christian hope will arrive when life finally triumphs over death and God's truth over worldly falsehood. Then every woe will be healed, for God "will wipe away every tear from their eyes; there shall be no more death, nor sorrow, nor crying. There shall be no more pain, for the former things have passed away" (Rev 21:4). "And those gathered by the Lord shall return and come to Zion with gladness, and with everlasting gladness over their heads" (Isa 35:9).

Here is the summit, crown, and full realization of Orthodox Christian hope and the triumph of those who, in this earthly life, were persecuted and oppressed and banished for Christ's truth.

POINTS OF REFLECTION

1. Why should loving parents not spoil their children?

2. What is Christian hope?

CHAPTER 13

The Education and Development of Man's Will

We must now examine the question of the training and development of man's will. The moral character and moral value of man's personality depend most of all on the direction and strength of the will. Of course, everyone understands that for a Christian it is necessary to have, first, a strong and decisive will, and second, a will that is firmly directed toward the good of the neighbor, toward the side of good and not evil.

How is one to develop a strong will? The answer is simple—above all through the exercise of the will. To do this, as with a bodily exercise, it is necessary to begin slowly, little by little. However, having begun to exercise one's will in anything (e.g., in a constant struggle with one's sinful habits or whims) this work on oneself must never cease. Moreover, a Christian who wishes to strengthen his will, his character, must from the very beginning avoid all dissipation, disorder, and inconsistency of behavior.

Otherwise, he will be a characterless person, not present-ing himself as anything definite. No one can rely on such an individual, neither other people nor even the person himself. In the Holy Scripture such a person is called a reed shaking in the wind.

Discipline is necessary for every one of us. It has such vital significance that without it, a correct, normal order and success in work is impossible. In the life of each indi-vidual it is of primary importance, for inner self-discipline takes the place of external school or military discipline here. Man must place himself in definite frameworks, having created well-defined conditions and an order of life, and not depart from these.

Let us note this, too: man's habits have a large signif-icance in the matter of strengthening the will. We have already seen that bad, sinful habits are a great obstacle for a Christian, moral life. On the other hand, good hab-its are a valuable acquisition for the soul and, therefore, man must teach himself much good so that what is good becomes his own, habitual. This is especially important in early years, when man's character is still forming. It is not in vain that we say that the second half of man's earthly life is formed from habits acquired in the first half of this life.

Probably no one would argue against the fact that man needs a strong will. In life we meet people with various degrees of strength of will. It often happens that a person who is very gifted, talented, with a strong mind and a profound good heart, turns out to be weak-willed and cannot carry out his plans in life, no matter how good and valuable they might be. On the contrary, it happens that a less-talented and less-gifted person, but one with a greater strength of will, stronger in character, succeeds in life.

A more important quality of the human will, however, is its correct direction to the side of good and not evil. If a good but weak-willed person can turn out to be of little use to society, then a person with a strong, but evil, destructive will is dangerous; and the stronger his evil will, the more dangerous he is. From this it is clear how extremely important are those principles, those basic foundations, and rules by which man's will is guided. An unprincipled man is a moral insignificance, not having any moral foundations, and dangerous for those around him.

From what source can man's will draw for itself these principles in order to act according to them? For an unbelieving person, an answer to this is extremely difficult and essentially impossible. Are they to be drawn from science? But science, in the first place, is interested primarily in questions of knowledge and not morals, and secondly, it does not contain anything solid and constant in principles, since it ceaselessly widens, deepens, and changes much. From philosophy? But philosophy itself teaches about the relativity and not any unconditional authenticity of its truths. From practical life? Even less. This life itself is in need of positive principles, which can purge it of unruly, unprincipled conditions.

Though the answer to the present question is so difficult for unbelievers, for a believing Christian the answer is simple and clear. The source of good principles is God's will. It is revealed to us in the Saviour's teaching, in His Holy Gospel. It alone has an unconditional steadfast authority in this area, and it alone has taught us self-sacrifice and Christian freedom, Christian equality, and brotherhood (an understanding stolen from it by those not of the Faith). The Lord Himself said of true Christians, "Not everyone who says to Me, 'Lord, Lord,' shall enter the kingdom of heaven, but he who does the will of My Father in heaven" (Matt 7:21).

POINTS OF REFLECTION

1. Just like our bodies our will needs to be exercised in order to develop. How is this done?

2. What is the primary source of godly principles for our will to conform to?

CHAPTER 14

Strengthening the Will with Work and Vows

Work is an indispensable characteristic of every virtue of man that strengthens his will. It is an obedience placed by God upon sinful man when he lost paradise: "In the sweat of your face you shall eat bread…" (Gen 3:19). Therefore, each one of us must work.

In the First Epistle to the Thessalonians, the apostle Paul wrote about the necessity of work: "We urge you, brethren … to mind your own business, and to work with your own hands, as we commanded you" (1 Thess 4:10–11). In the Second Epistle, he sharply rebuked those who act indecently and are superstitious, and he precisely sets forth his appeal to work: "If anyone will not work, neither shall he eat" (2 Thess 3:10). We must note here that Orthodoxy never divides work into "white collar" and "blue collar" work. Such divisions are accepted in contemporary society, which (although less so now) has tended to regard physical labor disdainfully. Orthodoxy requires only that a person's work be honorable and bring corresponding benefit. From an Orthodox Christian point of view, a person who treats his obligations disdainfully, although he is in a high and responsible post, is far lower than the most insignificant of his subordinates who fulfill their obligations conscientiously, in an Orthodox Christian manner. Moreover, one can easily discover through personal experience what a fulfilling satisfaction is felt by one who works honorably and well and what a squalid sediment remains in the soul after time spent in thoughtless emptiness.

A false and sinful view of work and amusement is becoming widespread in contemporary society. People look upon work as something very unpleasant, like a heavy, subjecting yoke, and they strive to remove themselves from it as quickly as possible. All their efforts are directed toward "rest" (from what?) and toward being amused. Firstly, this is sinful and completely not Christian. Secondly, there is a saying in Russian: "There is much time to work, one hour to rest." Many would like there to be several. Rest and amusement are pleasant and enjoyable only when they are earned by previous work. In order to prevent that emptiness and dissipation in the soul, which are so common now in our nervous, restless, vain times, an Orthodox Christian must learn to concentrate, to gather himself together. One must observe oneself in all respects and give oneself an account of one's moods and longings. One must also consider what must be done at any given moment and the aim toward which to direct one's efforts.

Speaking of strengthening the will, we must also remember those instances when a person feels that his will is powerless to withstand some temptation or sinful habit that has taken root. In such a case, one must remember that the first and basic means of resistance at such times is prayer, a humble prayer of faith and hope. More will be said about prayer further on. In the meantime, let us recall that even such a spiritually strong person as the apostle Paul spoke of his impotence to struggle with sin and do good: "For the good that I will to do, I do not do; but the evil I will not to do, that I practice" (Rom 7:19). How much more is it so with us then, who are ill and weak? But prayer can help us, since through it we receive God's almighty strength to help our powerlessness.

In addition to prayer, vows and oaths have a great significance in the strengthening of the will in the struggle with sin. A vow is a personal promise to do any good, beneficial deed, for example, to help a person in poverty, to build a church or public institution, to adopt an orphan, to make a pilgrimage, etc. When applied to our personal lives, such vows can consist of the following: if a person notices himself deficient in any way—not helpful to others, lazy, having little concern for the family, etc.—he must select a definite, constant good deed in this area and make himself fulfill it unfailingly, as his obligation. Oaths are negative vows. One gives an oath not to commit one or another sin, to struggle in the most resolute manner with one or another sinful habit (for example, to cease drinking, smoking, swearing, etc.). It is obvious that a person must give vows or oaths only after having assessed his strength and resolved that with God's help he will fulfill them, no matter what. The Saviour warns us against vows that are made carelessly, without thought and not according to our strength, in the parable about the unwise builder. In the parable, the man began grandly to build a tower but could not complete it and his neighbors laughed at him, saying, "This man began to build and was not able to finish?" (Luke 14:30).

If you have made a vow, then having called upon God's help, set yourself to fulfill it unwaveringly.

POINTS OF REFLECTION

1. Why is work important to our spiritual life?

2. What are some of the tools God has given us to confront habitual sin?

CHAPTER 15
The Struggle against Lust

Man consists of soul and body. Many ancient religions and philosophical teachings spoke of man's soul being created by God, while the body supposedly came from the evil principle—from the devil. Orthodoxy teaches otherwise. Both the soul and body of man are created by God. According to Apostolic teaching, after the mystery of baptism, man's body is a temple of the Holy Spirit, and the members of the body, through union with Christ in the mystery of Holy Communion, are members of Christ. Therefore, man will pass over into the future eternal blessedness (or into eternal torment) with his entire being, both the immortal soul, and the body that will be resurrected and reunited with the soul before Christ's judgment. This means that, while caring about one's soul, an Orthodox Christian must not leave the body without attention. One must guard it—guard it in an Orthodox way—not only from illnesses, but also from sins that corrupt, defile, and weaken it. Among such sins, the most dangerous and harmful is licentiousness, the loss of chastity and bodily purity.

It gives us no particular joy to bring up this subject, of which to a Christian, according to the words of the apostle Paul, it is "shameful to speak," but it is impossible not to mention it, since there is no sin more dangerous or horrible for youth—it is worse than an epidemic, worse than the plague.

We are speaking of fornication, of corruption, and of sexual degeneracy, which are without a doubt the most terrible wounds of contemporary mankind. It is difficult to enumerate the terrible consequences that follow after this sin, like an inseparable shadow. We will not speak of specific illnesses, which so often result from a disordered life, but most to be feared is the final judgment of Him Who commanded us to lead a pure and undefiled life—the Terrible Judgment, at which the apostle Paul said the Lord will condemn fornicators and adulterers (see Heb 13:4).

How is one who wishes to preserve oneself pure and chaste to struggle with the temptation of this sin? The answer is simple: first of all, by purity of thought and imagination. It is often claimed that sexual needs act with such insurmountable strength that man is powerless to withstand them. This is a falsehood. This is not a matter of "need" but of depravity and lechery and results from a person's unrestrained provoking of himself with thoughts and desires. Of course such a person builds upon the natural sexual inclination to an excessive degree and this brings him to sin. An Orthodox Christian, however, who is God-loving and strict with himself will never allow, never permit, bad desires and thoughts to possess his mind and heart. In order to accomplish this, he will call upon God's help in prayer and, with the sign of the Cross, struggle against such thoughts the instant they appear. By effort of the will one will bring one's thoughts over to prayer or at least to other more edifying subjects. If one allows oneself to be inflamed by impure imagination, it means that one has depraved and ruined oneself. In order to struggle with bad thoughts, an Orthodox person must firmly turn away from and quickly depart from all that can elicit these bad thoughts. Our Saviour was not speaking in vain when He so strictly warns us of the impure, "the lust of the eyes" (1 Jn 2:16)—and "the lust of the eyes" Christ warned us about went no further than looking. So dangerous is mental temptation (see Jas 1:13–17).

There are so many temptations: a general degeneration of morals and a departure from a pure, ordered Orthodox life, a disturbed and harmful relationship to marriage and married life—these cannot help but act upon the young soul. Added to this, there are motion pictures and literature vying with each other in praising sin and describing it in the most alluring colors, with such complete openness and shamelessness, that it would shock our modest and God-fearing ancestors. Contrived music, dances, and entertainments blind contemporary paganized "Christian" society so much that it no longer perceives their sinfulness and harmfulness. Various types of obscene humor are now quite acceptable in society. All this is a spiritual rottenness and pestilence, corrupting and killing the mind and heart of man—all this cloud of temptations moves among the young, developing soul of humanity.

Blessed is the one who from youth to the end of his days has remained pure in body and soul. Blessed is the one who has brought, with the fragrant freshness, the strength of the untouched power of the soul and body into the bright union of marriage blessed by God and the Church, or who has preserved all this to the grave in the radiant purity of virginity and chastity! God blesses only two paths for man on earth: either the holy path of Christian marriage, an indissoluble union of two hearts, or else a higher and holier path, a path of virginity, a consecration of oneself to God and neighbors—holy monasticism.

Terrible is the end of the path of him who disdains, ignores, and stubbornly violates the laws of Christian purity and righteousness given by God, thus defiling the body and killing the soul. For him, either sooner or later, will be fulfilled the fearful sentence: "Vengeance is Mine, I will repay, says the Lord" (Rom 12:19).

POINTS OF REFLECTION

1. Why should we live a chaste life?

2. What two paths are given to us by God for living a chaste life?

CHAPTER 16

Drunkenness, Greed, and Other Carnal Problems; Christian Death

Of the other "conditions of the flesh," that is, sins that have taken deep root in the very nature of man, perhaps the most dangerous is drunkenness and drug addiction. This sin is very widespread now. Let everyone remember that one must not wait until this ruinous passion has already developed, but one must guard oneself against it before it develops, when it is significantly easier. We already know how much easier it is for a person to struggle with the temptation of sin when it has not yet become, through repetition, a lasting habit. It is better not to drink at all, from youth on. Youth has much vivacity and sufficient energy without it, and to "warm oneself with vodka" is so unnecessary. A proverb says, "Give the demon a finger and it will take the whole hand." The will power of young people is not yet strong, but the temptations of drink or drugs are numerous.

Many are ruined in early years by a peculiar type of "courage," a type of sportive passion wherein a person wants to "prove" his strength and steadiness in the use of alcoholic drinks. Of course, one would show far greater steadiness and strength—real moral strength—if he could really control himself and not yield to this evil temptation. An Orthodox person must, by all measures, draw away from sinful seductions and remove them from himself, remembering how the apostle warns that bad associations deprave good morals (1 Cor 15:33; 2 Thess 3:6).

There is another carnal sin that, at first glance, does not seem as ruinous as drunkenness and depravity, but which is, nevertheless, extremely dangerous. This is the sin of the love of money. The apostle Paul says literally that the love of money is the root of all kinds of evil (1 Tim 6:10). The first danger for a person who has egoistically acquired wealth is that this very wealth opens the access to all other seductions of the world. Moreover, the wealth itself becomes that idol (exactly as the golden idol did [see Exodus chapter 32]) to which man adheres with all his soul and heart, becoming unable to tear himself away from service to it. We see an example of this in the Gospel story about the rich young man who could not follow the Saviour because his life was bound to his wealth. In this regard, Christ said that "it is hard for a rich man to enter the kingdom of heaven" (Matt 19:23). Thus does wealth blind a man and make him its slave. This danger threatens everyone who becomes addicted to "acquiring," to seeking gain and aiming for it.

In order to prevent this vice of loving money from developing in a person, it is necessary to teach him Christian unselfishness in his early years. All the works of an Orthodox Christian must be done unselfishly or, as it says in Scripture, "for Christ's sake" (2 Cor 12:10; see also 1 Cor 4:10). As we mentioned earlier, according to Divine truth, the Gospel truth, it is not the person that saves possessions for himself who acquires, but rather it is the one who gives to others in the work of giving mercy and alms to his neighbors who makes gains. The one who serves others in the struggle of good not only shows them Orthodox Christian help but also benefits his own soul, acquiring for himself a true treasure in heaven.

A person who is seeking to lead an Orthodox life should not be negligent about his health. Health is a valuable gift from God and should be guarded. It is foolish to assume that a Christian should not seek to be cured by doctors. Doctors and medicines exist by God's will. We read in the Scripture that the Lord created certain things for curative use. Orthodoxy, however, sees in illness the direct consequences of our sinfulness. For this reason, a believing person begins his treatment first of all with prayer, with the purification and strengthening of the soul, with the Holy Mysteries. Then he follows the treatment of the body prescribed by a doctor. We can see this pattern in the

Gospel where, before healing a person from his physical illness, Christ healed his soul with the forgiveness of sins. To one, the Saviour said, "Behold, thou art made whole: sin no more, lest a worse thing come unto thee" (John 5:14).

While giving attention to his health, an Orthodox person must not fear death. We are not speaking of the martyr's death for Christ's sake, which every believer desires with joy, but simply of the end of our earthly life. True Orthodox Christians in general do not fear death, but even await it hopefully. The apostle Paul, for example, says directly, "[I have] a desire to depart and be with Christ, which is far better" than remaining on earth (Phil 1:23). In another place he says that we have home in heaven (see 2 Cor 5:1–3), teaching us that our true native land is there, while on earth, we are only temporary exiles. That longed for "Christian end of our life" is not always without illness but in any case is "blameless and peaceful." One prepares for such an end by prayer, contemplation, and partaking of the Holy Mysteries. We should not think that only those who are dying need to partake of the Holy Mysteries. Everyone who is seriously sick needs to partake of the Holy Mysteries, for the healing of soul and body, considering them to be the best medicine.

A shameful, non-Christian death, on the other hand, is a terrible thing, for example, a crook dying in the middle of a crime, and so forth. At this point, we must mention suicide. It is well known that the Holy Church by its canons withholds a Christian burial to those who consciously (without mental impairment) take their own lives. Suicide is a complete betrayal of the very spirit of Christianity, a refusal to bear one's cross, a rejection of God and hope in Him. Suicide is the sordid death of the complete egoist, thinking only of himself, not thinking of others or his responsibilities to them. In the Gospel we see the first suicide to be Judas the betrayer, who terribly and shamefully ended his life. One who commits suicide ceases to be a faithful son of the Holy Church and thus deprives himself of his burial. And how could the Church bury a suicide according to Her service? The main thought of this burial service is "Give rest, O Lord, to the soul of Thy servant, for he placed his hope in Thee." But these words will ring with untruth in the case of a suicide. How could the Holy Church affirm untruth?

POINTS OF REFLECTION

1. What is the benefit of confronting a sin at an early stage of temptation?

2. How does secular medicine work together with faith in God?

∾ CHAPTER 17
Christian Justice

U p to this point, we have talked about the duties of a Christian in relation to himself. Now, let us examine his obligations in relation to others.

The first element for a proper relationship with other people is justice. Without this basic element, even one's goodness can turn out to be useless—if partiality and one-sidedness appear in it instead of truth. There are, however, marked differences in the conditions of just relationships between people. Legal or Loyal Justice (from the French): This is the lowest form of just relationship, the most widespread in civil and state life. A loyal person strives to precisely fulfill state and civil laws, which are mandatory for him and for others. In addition, he usually fulfills all his personal transactions and obligations exactly and punctually. He does not, however, go a step further than these legal norms and boundaries, to make concessions and adaptations. This type of person can be cold, unsympathetic, and pitiless. Such a person of iniquity neither creates nor violates laws—but will take what is his own without concessions, even if his neighbor will suffer from this. Of course, in our time such legally just persons are comparatively orderly, since they fulfill their obligations honorably. For an Orthodox Christian, nevertheless, it is clear that such a relationship is insufficient because it is not Christian but purely pagan.

Justice of Correctness: In respect to morality, this form of justice is significantly higher than the previous one. We refer to a person as correct who, in his relationships with those around him, strives to fulfill what is necessary not only according to external laws and customs, but also according to his conscience. Therefore, he treats everyone equally and is peaceful, polite, and considerate toward everyone. He willingly responds to a request for help and tries to do everything that he has promised, often freeing other people from difficulties by this. In comparison to legalistically loyal people, it is easy and pleasant to live and work with such correct, conscientious persons. Still, this is far from Christianity since such compassion and such responsiveness is seldom constant and faithful to itself, and it reaches a point where it fades and dries up. Then such a person, while perhaps outwardly remaining correct and proper in his relationships with people, usually tries to quickly and politely excuse himself and refuse their requests and needs.

Christian justice: This is the complete type of justice—
the justice of the Christian heart. Its basic, wise, clear, and
comprehensible principle is expressed in the Gospel by
the words: "Therefore, whatever you want men to do to
you, do also to them" (Matt 7:12). And the Apostolic Council repeated this in a negative form: "Do not do to others
what you do not wish done to yourself" (Acts 15:29 in the
Slavonic text[1]). And so do not bring about any falsehood or
lie or offense or evil. All people are your neighbors; do not
do to them what you do not wish for yourself. Moreover,
not only must we do no evil, but we must do good, according to our conscience, from the heart, being motivated by
the Gospel law of love, mercy, and forgiveness. If you
want people to treat you sincerely, then open your heart to
your neighbors. Do not be an egoist, do not consider your
rights as legalistic and correct people do; rather place the
welfare and good of your neighbors above all your rights,
according to the law of Christian love.

It very often happens in life that we are too condescending to ourselves but are too demanding and strict with
neighbors. Christian justice speaks otherwise. The Lord
said: "And why do you look at the speck in your brother's eye, but do not consider the plank in your own eye?
Or how can you say to your brother ... Hypocrite! First
remove the plank from your own eye, and then you will
see clearly to remove the speck from your brother's eye"
(Matt 7:3, 5). For this reason, ascetics of Christianity, while

grieving so about their own sins, being almost pitilessly strict and demanding of themselves, were so all-forgiving and compassionate to others, covering the faults of their neighbors with kindness and love. In general, the Christian rule of life teaches us that in such sorrowful events as arguments and misunderstanding we must not seek to find guilt in others, but in ourselves, in our own lusts, obduracy, self-love, and egoism. Thus, Christian justice demands from us condescension toward others. Even this, however, is not sufficient. It calls us to see in every person, our own brother, a brother in Christ, a beloved creation and image of All-Mighty God. And no matter how a man might fall, no matter how he darkens the image of God in himself by sins and vices, we must still seek the spark of God in his soul. "Sins are sins, but the basis in man is God's image ... Hate sin, but love the sinner," St John of Kronstadt once said.

Together with respect for the person of our neighbor, we must also exhibit trust in him. This is especially necessary when a person who has fallen into error comes forth with the evangelical words, "I repent," and promises correction. How often the good intention of such a repenting person is met with mistrust and coldness, and the good desire for correction disappears, being replaced by anger and a destructive decision? "Well then just you wait ... I'll show you ... I'll get you." Who answers for the destruction of this soul? A sincere, loving Christian, on the contrary, joyfully receives the good volition of his neighbor, emphasizing his full trust and respect toward the one repenting and by this often supporting and strengthening on the right path one who is still weak and faltering. Of course, it sometimes happens that a person who has promised to correct himself will, either through weakness of will or through a conscious desire to deceive, misuse the trust of the neighbor. But can this crush the feeling of trust and goodwill toward his neighbor in a believing Christian? For he is a son and disciple of the law of Christian love, which the apostle Paul said "bears all things, believes all things, hopes all things, endures all things" (1 Cor 13:7).

POINTS OF REFLECTION

1. What does justice consist of for a Christian?

2. Should we accept all persons' repentance as genuine or perhaps reject them?

CHAPTER 18

Falsehood: Christian Charity

One of the most important defects of contemporary society is falsehood. It is made manifest in various forms, especially in the usual form of lying in general conversation and in the form of deceit in business life. It is extremely dangerous to view this sin lightly, which is now encountered everywhere. It is considered quite usual to confirm something whether or not one knows it to be true; to say, "We will not be home," to avoid a guest or caller; to claim to be ill, while being healthy, etc. (to this we must add false "compliments," flattery, praise, etc.) People forget that falsehood is from the devil, of whom Christ the Saviour said that he is "a liar and the father of [lies]" (John 8:44). Thus, every liar is a co-worker and instrument of the devil. Already in the Old Testament we are told, "Lying lips are an abomination to the Lord" (Prov 12:24 LXX).

Falsehood in the form of gossip or slander is especially dangerous. Everyone knows what gossip is—a net of seduction and falsehood, woven by the devil, which entangles and darkens the good relationship of people among themselves. This gossip—the child of falsehood and idle talk—has become the favorite part of almost all conversation. Still worse and direr is slander, that is, a conscious falsehood against a person with the aim of harming him. This type of falsehood is singularly devilish, for the very word "devil" means "slanderer."

When our Lord Jesus Christ reproached the scribes and Pharisees, He usually called them hypocrites, by this indicating that dire form of falsehood—hypocrisy—with which these so-called leaders of the people were filled. The Pharisees outwardly seemed to be saints, but in their hearts and souls, they were malicious haters of truth and good. For this reason, the Lord likened them to finely finished coffins, which are beautiful on the outside, but within are full of dead bones and corruption. The vice of hypocrisy is widespread even now in the form of pretending and desiring to seem to be what one is not—not to be, but to seem. A Christian strives, of course, not to seem, but to be good. This is not easy and often passes almost unnoticed by anyone, except for the All-seeing God. And many—especially among the youth—try to seem cleverer, more beautiful, more gifted, more developed, and more charitable than they are in reality. From this, they obtain that mortal deceit and insincerity, which now so often destroys people and their happiness, which are clearly based on falsehood and not on truth.

We have already mentioned that the basis of a Christian's relationship with his neighbors is love, and thus he strives to do good to them and for them. One who does not do good is not a Christian. And this good, this love toward neighbors, must definitely be expressed in works of mercy and goodwill toward everyone. It is not without reason that the Saviour commanded us to love not only those who love us, but also those who hate us. Moreover, in His conversation about the Dread Judgment, He clearly indicated what it is that will be asked of us first and above all at the Judgment. Neither wealth, nor glory, nor education will have any significance there. The basis of the Dread Judgment will be the question, terrible and fateful for egotists and self-lovers: "How did you serve your neighbors?" Christ enumerates six particular forms of physical help. In His love, compassion, and mercy, He identifies Himself with every unfortunate person and with all those in need of help "for I was hungry and you gave Me food; I was thirsty and you gave Me drink; I was a stranger and you took Me in; I was naked and you clothed Me; I was sick and you visited Me; I was in prison and you came to Me" (Matt 25:35–36). And St John Chrysostom pointedly says, "This image of love is broad and this command is wide." Indeed, the command concerning mercy encompasses the entirety of man's life, and many times the Lord revealed to His Saints that deeds of mercy and compassion cover a person's most serious sins. Of course, Christian help is not limited to deeds of physical help. Equally, there is spiritual help—which is often immeasurably more important and valuable. Sometimes, for a despondent person, a simple word of sincere compassion, comfort, and understanding is dearer than any material support. Who would argue against the fact that one cannot value, in terms of money, the service of saving a person by means of sincere compassion and gentle words from, for example, the vice of drunkenness or the sin of suicide? The apostle James wrote concerning such precious spiritual help, "He who turns a sinner from the error of his way will save a soul from death [both the sinner's and his own] and cover a multitude of sins" (Jas 5:20).

In concluding these words about the duty of charity to neighbors, let us explain the difference between personal charity and social charity. Examples of the first are the giving of alms to a blind person or to a beggar, adopting poor orphans, etc. Examples of the second are founding charitable societies, temperance societies, societies to aid education, refuges for children, the ill or the aged, etc. Without a doubt, charity is a preeminent virtue as our Lord made clear in the Gospel. Such personal help can create a highly Christian relationship of participation, gratitude, and mutual love. This kind of direct charity can, however, provide opportunities for people who misuse it by constantly begging or employing deceit and dishonesty. This does not occur in a social charity that is not administered by chance but is planned and organized, bringing many substantial benefits. Of course, in this form of charity, there are far fewer of those vital bonds of personal love and trust such as are formed in cases of personal help, but then, each person who gives a donation here knows that he is participating in a vital Christian way in something truly serious and valuable.

POINTS OF REFLECTION

1. What are some of the most serious manifestations of the sin of falsehood in a person's life?

2. For what will we be judged on Judgment Day?

CHAPTER 19

Envy; Cursing and Anger

When the Lord talked with the Apostles about the last times He said that then, because iniquity shall abound, "the love of many shall grow cold" (Matt 24:12). It would seem that this prophecy is being fulfilled already in our days—days of mutual alienation and coldness of relationships. This is especially noticeable now that the enemies of Christ's faith are planting envy and ill will in the masses, in place of Christ's love and goodwill. And our Saviour included envy in the category of serious sins. By its very essence, envy is impossible in people who are of a Christian disposition. For, in every good family, envy is impossible as all members of the family rejoice over (rather than envy) the success of any one of its members. This must be the case in the relationships of all Orthodox Christians, a family, as children of one loving Heavenly Father. Therefore, the apostle Paul calls upon us not only to commiserate with those who are weeping, but also to rejoice with those who are rejoicing, as opposed to those who envy the successes of others. In order to free oneself from feelings of envy, one must recall that one's own vanity and egoistic competitiveness are the basis of this sinful feeling. In their egoism, people usually fear that they will not be recognized, will not be given their "due," and others will be placed higher than they, etc. The Christian fears the reverse—he fears being placed higher than others and offending them.

Together with envy, a strong enemy of good relationships between people is speaking evil at various times: speaking falsely, argumentativeness, abusive speech. How strange it is that people have become so numb and blind that they consider all these sins as nothing and do not even take notice of the constant sin in speaking evil. But here is what the apostle James says of these "sins of the tongue": "See how great a forest a little fire kindles! And the tongue is a fire, a world of iniquity … an unruly evil, full of deadly poison" (Jas 3:5, 8). And again he says that "if anyone among you thinks he is religious, and does not bridle his tongue but deceives his own heart, this one's religion is useless" (Jas 1:26). The Lord, moreover, pointedly said that "by your words you will be justified, and by your words you will be condemned" (Matt 12:37). So dangerous are the sins of the word!

The most repulsive of these sins of speaking evil is undoubtedly the sordid and repulsive habit of unprintable swearing—to which so many are now subject. What a shame this is, what sordidness, what an insult to the purity and chastity that the Lord expects of us and has commended to us. Yet many people think that all this is "nonsense," "of no consequence," forgetting about those fearsome words: "By your words you will be justified, and by your words you will be condemned" (Matt 12:37), which we have already cited. The apostle James asks, "Does a spring send forth fresh water and biter from the same opening?" (Jas 3:11). But we, nevertheless, profane our lips with this repulsive swearing and imagine that fragrant words of pure prayer to God will flow through these very same lips, and with these profaned and dirtied lips we accept the holiest of all holy things, the most pure Mysteries of Christ. No, "put off all these; anger, wrath, malice, blasphemy, filthy language out of your mouth" (Col 3:8)—whoever has ears to hear, let him hear!

In contradiction to all these sources of mutual anger and arguments, Christianity calls us to be peace loving and forgiving of all offenses. Again we turn to the commandments of blessedness: "Blessed are the meek, for they shall inherit the earth .... Blessed are the peacemakers, for they shall be called sons of God" (Matt 5:5–10). A meek person is above all an amiable and simple person and an unwavering opponent of all egoism. There is within him no self-satisfaction or self-interest. On the contrary, he seeks first of all what is beneficial for others, not for himself.

While most egotists usually appear as a pack of hungry wolves, outbidding one another in efforts to seize upon the prey, snatching it away from one another, meek people yield to everyone and help in everything. It is worthy of note that, according to the Gospel, this type of behavior is the most straightforward and most stable; for it is no one else but they, the meek, who will inherit the earth, even though they pass through this life like sheep among wolves, according to the clear image of our Saviour.

Still more exalted is the virtue of peace-making. And the reward for it is higher—Divine: "for they shall be called sons of God." The Christian peacemaker is, by this deed, like the first "Peacemaker"—the Son of God, during whose birth the angels sang: "And on earth peace, goodwill toward men!" (Luke 2:14). The meek person creates an atmosphere of comfort and peace around himself and does not anger others. The peacemaker strives to spread this atmosphere of peace and good relationships as widely as possible, and he strives to reconcile others. Such a struggle demands great spiritual exertion, patience, and a readiness to meet a cold lack of understanding, derision, enmity, and resistance. A Christian peacemaker, however, is always ready for all this, since he knows that every Christian struggle to do good is higher and of greater value the more it encounters difficulties and resistance.

The Gospel virtue of long suffering is organically bound with meekness and peace-making and must be a distinguishing feature of every Christian. It is manifested most of all in the forgiveness of personal offenses and insults, as the Saviour commanded us, saying: "Whoever slaps you on your right cheek, turn the other to him also" (Matt 5:39). In other words, do not respond to violence with violence, but respond to evil with good. And the apostle Paul explains: "If your enemy is hungry, feed him; If he is thirsty, give him a drink; For in so doing you will heap coals of fire on his head." "Do not be overcome by evil, but overcome evil with good" (Rom 12:20–21). And the reverse: if a person responds to evil with evil, then he has evidently become a prisoner of this evil and is defeated by it (of course, we are speaking of personal offenses). In life, we repeatedly observe that a person who is offended by someone becomes angry and even takes revenge. But revenge is, beyond a doubt, a sin, and for a Christian it is unacceptable. "Beloved, do not avenge not yourselves," appeals the apostle Paul (Rom 12:19). Revenge is a complete betrayal of the Christian spirit of meekness and forgiveness and it shows the absence of Christian love in a person.

The situation is somewhat different in the matter of anger. The Lord did not forbid it as a sin except for anger "in vain." And the apostle says, "Be angry, and do not sin" (Eph 4:26), thus indicating that anger can also not be sinful. The Lord Jesus Christ Himself was angered by the falseness and stubbornness of the Pharisees (see Mark 3:5). Thus anger can be naturally lawful and just. It was with such anger that St Nicholas the Wonderworker was stirred when, at the First Ecumenical Council, he struck the blasphemous heretic Arius on the cheek. This anger came from a pure source, fervent zealousness for the glory of God. Anger is sinful when, firstly, it is unjust and vain. This often happens when one is faced with the truth and it strikes one's egoism and self-love. St John of Kronstadt advises us not only not to be angry at those who offend our self-love, but to value them as spiritual doctors who reveal the sores of our proud and vainglorious soul. Still, anger that has a just beginning can become sinful when a person intentionally utilizes it with an unkind heart. Then a person attunes his own heart to anger and by this he undoubtedly sins. Speaking against this, the apostle says: "Do not let not the sun go down on your wrath" (Eph 4:26). Consciously thought out and retained anger can pass over into spitefulness, which is so opposed to the spirit of Christian love.

POINTS OF REFLECTION

1. What is envy a manifestation of?

2. What are the characteristics of a peacemaker?

3. Is anger always a sin? If not, why not?

CHAPTER 20

Insolvent Ethical Systems

I t is easy to see that all the qualities of a Christian relationship with one's neighbors—meekness, peace-making, long suffering, etc.—lead us to one basic and fundamental virtue. This virtue is Christian love, and it is the basis of Christian morality.

In addition to the moral system offered by Orthodox Christianity, there are also non-Christian, secular moral systems. While they agree in many points with the teaching of Christian morality, these systems nevertheless do not acknowledge the principle of Christian love as the basic teaching about morality. They seem to be frightened by the high degree of love commanded by the Gospel, and they seek principles for themselves, which are easier and more acceptable.

Of these secular systems of morality, the best known and most widely spread in practical life are eudemonism and utilitarianism. For eudemonism (epicureanism), the basis of morality is man's personal striving for happiness. Moreover, it understands happiness as the sum of the satisfactions and enjoyments from which one's life becomes pleasant. Eudemonists, nevertheless, differ in their opinions of precisely what satisfactions one must seek in order to be happy. Some of them (if not the majority) speak almost exclusively, of course, of sensual satisfactions. The apostle Paul described the basic ideal of such eudemonism as "Let us eat and drink; for tomorrow we die" (1 Cor 15:32).

Other eudemonists, pointing out that enthusiasm for sensual satisfactions destroys one's body and soul, recommend that one not be captivated by them. They advise that one ought rather to obtain satisfactions that are more stable and of longer duration, and also more spiritualized. Such, for example, are music, poetry, and various types of art and science in general.

Naturally, neither form of eudemonism is an acceptable principle of morality for Orthodox Christians. The fundamental question of morality is the difference between good and evil, between what is good and what is bad. Eudemonism, however, speaks of what is pleasant and what is unpleasant. No one could argue the point that these are far from being one and the same thing. Clearly, eudemonistic people will, in practical life, always be egotists who willfully demand and take what is pleasant for themselves, refusing what is unpleasant (even when acting otherwise might be pleasant and beneficial to others).

Moreover, what morality can we speak of in a situation where all people are endeavoring to obtain only that which they like?

When viewed from the strictly Orthodox Christian point of view, eudemonism becomes even more insolvent and positively absurd. Orthodoxy constantly turns one's thoughts to the immortality of the soul and to accounting at the Last Judgment for one's earthly life and behavior. What awaits the eudemonistic egoist at the Judgment from Him Who will question them concerning their love and help for their suffering brother? Their lot will be the fate of the rich man in the parable of the rich man and Lazarus. It cannot be otherwise since a fundamental and well-known principle of Christianity is: "Enter by the narrow gate; for wide is the gate and broad is the way that leads to destruction, and there are many who go in by it. Because narrow is the gate and difficult is the way which leads to life, and there are few who find it" (Matt 7:13–14).

Utilitarianism (a philosophy of the common good) is a somewhat better system of non-Christian morality. This system enjoins one to do what is beneficial, rather than what is pleasant, for one. Even so, this moral system cannot be called justifiable. The concept of "beneficial" seldom coincides with the concept of "good" as something absolutely good. Medicine, for example, is beneficial in restoring health, but at the same time, weapons—a revolver or a knife—are beneficial to a thief in the fulfillment of his evil intent. Thus, the principle of usefulness or beneficialness cannot be established as a basis of morality. If we express this utilitarian principle in a concise form, "Act in a way that is beneficial (i.e., advantageous) to you," then it is clear that here again we have the elevation of that same coarse egoism, which we have already mentioned. It can be strait tight, narrow, strict, rigorous; a narrow, difficult place of passage.

For this reason, some utilitarian philosophers strive to soften this ideal by recommending that one pursue not only one's own personal advantage, but the common good, common benefit in which, they claim, the personal good of each individual is to be found. In this case, utilitarianism appears to be a more ennobled and lofty form. It nevertheless remains insufficient unless it is supported by the lofty principles of Christianity. First, its main shortcoming is the fact that the concepts of "useful" and "good" do not necessarily coincide. Secondly, there are situations in practical life in which one can be restrained from crime only by religious feelings—fear to violate the law of Highest Truth—but not by the dry rationale of utilitarianism. For example, a hungry man is faced with a temptation to steal bread or money from a neighbor. What can prevent him from doing this? Utilitarianism cannot give one moral support when one is wavering on the edge of temptation. Let the utilitarian teach him to seek not his own good but the common good, since his personal good is included in the common good. But then, if in the name of this "common good" he does not steal money or bread, he could perish from starvation. Where then is his personal good? In death from starvation?

Thus, Orthodox Christians can in no way view either eudemonism or utilitarianism as justifiable systems of morality. These systems are now very widely developed, but we must note nevertheless that their adherents are often completely orderly people. Why? Because the morality and opinions and views of society today still bear the imprint of the influence of Christianity after many centuries. Christianity has made a strong impression on mankind. It is only because of this that people who consider themselves to be eudemonists or utilitarians can, in real life, be honorable and orderly. They have grown up and have been nurtured with purely Christian, moral, and exalted ideas and therefore, in many respects they remain Christians in spirit, and even unwittingly, their utilitarianism and eudemonistic ideas are often cloaked in a mantle of Christian idealism.

POINTS OF REFLECTION

1. Can we say that the pursuit of happiness is a worthy goal for a Christian?

2. Why does the idea of the common good fall short of Christian love?

CHAPTER 21

Christian Love as the Basic Principle of Morality

We have observed that those systems of morality that do not found themselves upon the Gospel teaching of love are unjustifiable. We have also observed that Christian morality is completely established on the law of love; this law is the foundation and crown.

What, exactly, is this Christian love? In its fully developed state, it is the most elevated, powerful, and radiant of all human feelings. It is manifested as an experience of especially spiritual and moral closeness, of a most strong inner gravitation of one person to another. The heart of a loving person is open to the one who is loved, and is ready to receive him to itself, and ready to give itself to the other. "O Corinthians!" the apostle Paul wrote to his beloved spiritual children, "We have spoken openly to you, our heart is wide open" (2 Cor 6:11). "By this all will know that you are My disciples, if you have love for one another"

(John 13:35), said the Lord Jesus Christ to His Apostles (and through them to all of us).

Christian love is a special feeling, which draws one near to God Who is love itself, in the words of His beloved apostle (1 Jn 4:8). In the sphere of earthly feelings, there is no love higher than a love that is ready for self-sacrifice. And the whole history of God's relationship to man is a continuous history of the self-sacrifice of Heavenly love. The Heavenly King leads the sinner—the one who has opposed and betrayed Him—by the hand to salvation. For the sake of the sinner's salvation, He does not spare even His Only Begotten Son. The Son of God came down from heaven, became incarnate, suffered and died so that He, through the Resurrection, could give the sinner that blessed eternity, which he had lost by his own betrayal. Before His sufferings, moreover, He gave His faithful a final instruction, a commandment and ideal of love: "As I have loved you ... you also love one another" (John 13:34).

Such is the ideal of selfless Christian love. It embraces everyone, not just friends, but also enemies. In the Gospel, the Lord pointedly says: "If you love those who love you, what credit is that to you? For even sinners love those who love them" (Luke 6:32). By these words, the Lord warns us against the egoistically selfish character of non-Christian, pagan love. In such egoist love, the main element is our personal "I," our self-gratification, which we receive from this feeling. The Lord commanded something else of Christians: "Love your enemies, do good to those who hate you, bless those who curse you, and pray for those who spitefully use you" (Luke 6:27).

Thus, a Christian loves other people, not for their good or obliging disposition but for themselves; they are dear to him in themselves and the Christian's love seeks their salvation, even if they treat him as an enemy.

Perhaps nowhere in the Holy Scripture is the essence and nature of Christian love so clearly revealed as in Chapter 13 of the apostle Paul's First Epistle to the Corinthians. This chapter is appropriately called "the hymn of Christian love." Here, the apostle compares Christian love with various spiritual gifts and virtues. He calls love "a more excellent way" (1 Cor 12:31) and then explains, with unshakable conviction, how much higher it is than all the gifts and experiences of man.

"Though I speak with the tongues of men and of angels, but have not love," the apostle says, "I have become sounding brass or a clanging cymbal" (1 Cor 13:1) (like spiritless objects that act only on the external senses of man and not on his heart). And all the higher gifts and virtues—prophecy, understanding of all mysteries, wonderworking, faith, and even struggles of self-denial and martyrdom—without love they are nothing, and only from love do they acquire their worth.

"Love suffers long and is kind; love does not envy; love does not parade itself, is not puffed up; does not behave rudely" (1 Cor 13:4–5). It makes one patient, meek, humble, and benevolent toward everyone.

"Love suffers long and is kind; love does not envy; love does not parade itself, is not puffed up; does not behave rudely, does not seek its own, is not provoked, thinks no evil; does not rejoice in iniquity, but rejoices in the truth" (1 Cor 13:45–46). This is a victorious force, the power of humble love, which destroys the egoism and evil, which nest in man's heart. This true love always seeks truth and righteousness and not falsehood and obsequiousness. Finally, love "bears all things, believes all things, hopes all things, endures all things. Love never fails" (1 Cor 13:7–8).

Truly, never. Nothing will break it, neither trials nor torments, nor sorrow, nor deprivations, nor disenchantment. And it will go with a Christian to a new and better world where it will blossom in all its fullness when all other gifts have disappeared, and faith and hope have already ceased. Faith will be replaced by the sight of the reality, "face to face," and hope will come to realization; love alone will reign "unto ages of ages, forever." And thus, the same apostle says, "Love is the fulfillment of the law" (Rom 13:10).

POINTS OF REFLECTION

1. What do we most need to draw near to God and why?

2. Why is true love greater than faith and hope?

CHAPTER 22

The Orthodox Family

The basic task of Orthodox Christianity is to teach people to live according to God's will so that, through it, they will be brought to eternal blessedness. Some people vainly wish to reduce Christianity to a mere narrowly individualized sphere of religious experiences. Christianity, however, is life; it is a new seal on all the vital relationships of people. And no impartial person would doubt or contradict the fact of its influence on life. It is sufficient to point out that even though life and the behavior of people on earth have now strayed far from Christian ideals, nevertheless, their concepts and views were formulated on the Christian model. The work of many of the best artists and scientists bears a clearly Christian imprint upon them. Furthermore, such consoling phenomena as the disappearance of slavery, the appearance of a whole series of institutions of charity and enlightenment, and much else are undoubtedly obligated to Christianity for their beginnings. But perhaps, the transforming and elevating influence of Christianity has been experienced most of all by the primary unit in the structure of social life—the family.

It is a great responsibility for an Orthodox Christian person to choose a friend for life. God's word says of the Christian marriage, "The two shall become one flesh" (Gen 2:24), that is, in marriage, two people form one organism, one common life. An Orthodox Christian wife thinks first of all about her husband and then about herself. Likewise, the husband first cares for his wife and then for himself. The Lord tempered such a Christian marital union by His Divine word, "therefore what God has joined together, let not man separate" (Matt 19:6). It is noteworthy that in such a Christian marriage, the love of the partners has that very same self-less, self-denying character by which purely Christian love is distinguished. With good reason, the apostle Paul compares the marital union with the union of Christ and the Church, and he says, "Husbands, love your wives, just as Christ also loved the church and gave Himself for her" (Eph 5:25). In Christian marriage, the unification of loving personalities becomes so all-comprehensive and full, the mutual dedication of the spouses so deep and absolute, that they resemble each other in everything, and sometimes in old age they even come to resemble each other externally. And their life passes in full accord, in full dedication to the will of Christ the Saviour and His Holy Church.

But it becomes so sorrowful in our own days to see the precipitous, unthinkingly careless, and completely un-Christian disposition of contemporary youth to this most serious question. One must now repeatedly observe how marriages are concluded not through a serious, deep, examined feeling of love, but through amorousness, a feeling that is not serious, and is shallow, and morally very low. Often, the content of such an enamored state is, alas, in essence only animal passions, only an "agitation of young blood" (and sometimes not young, but old and seething with filth). Together with this, in the prenuptial time of such "marriages," one constantly observes deceit and self-embellishing of both body and soul, a hypocritical desire not to be, but to seem to be better and more beautiful. Life, however, can be built only on truth; it cannot survive on falsehood. From this, there ensues the disenchantment of spouses with each other and disgraceful practices. Who does not know that in these days these couples "in love" continually end up in civil marriages? These are unlawful unions, systematic and continual violations of the seventh Commandment, for which the Church forbids them to receive the Holy Mysteries. Nearly always they end tragically—not only in arguments, but with crimes, murder, and suicide.

Christian marriage is a single life lived by two in unification. With the years, marital life only strengthens, becomes deeper, more spiritual. Of course, passionate love, connected with each person's natural sexual inclination and purely physical attraction, also enters into Christian marital love. In a truly Christian marriage, however, such passionate love enters into the attachment only incidentally and never has such a significance and strength as in non-Christian marital unions. In the lives of Saints, we see a multitude of examples in which Christian spouses, through mutual agreement, renounced sexual life, either from the very beginning of the marriage or even after forty years. It is noteworthy that in such a marriage, when the ascetic spouses live "as brother and sister," their mutual love is distinguished by a special strength of devotion, all-embracing fidelity, and mutual respect. Thus does Christianity consecrate, elevate, and transform a marriage union.

In a Christian family, not only the relationship of husband and wife is considered, but also that of children and parents. Christianity again places its imprint on this interrelationship.

In each good family there must, without fail, be a single family life. "Our" must always take precedence over the personal "my" in such a relationship. It is not in vain that all members of the family bear one common surname, for they must live a common, cordial life. The head of the family is the husband. The well-being of the family is formed on him and on his toils. The family is his first duty. Of those who do not look after their own family, the apostle Paul says bluntly and quite clearly: "But if anyone does not provide for his own, and especially for those of his household, he has denied the faith and is worse than an unbeliever" (1 Tim 5:8).

It often happens that, in directing their children to one or another path, parents act so strongly against the will of a child's inclinations and heart's desire that they are generally unjust. The apostle Paul speaks against this, pointedly saying: "Fathers, do not provoke your children to wrath [lest they be discouraged]" (Col 3:21), "but bring them up in the training and admonition of the Lord" (Eph 6:4).

To demand of children what exceeds their strength only plunges them into despondency. There is an even greater injustice: for a child, the father is the highest authority, and woe to the father if his authority betrays that feeling of trust, a feeling that is far stronger in a child than in an adult. This is followed by a situation that is simply inescapable for the child. It is even worse, however, when the parents spoil their children too much, are too condescending toward them, and often leave them without supervision. The child can receive great moral ruin from this; as we have seen, God's word orders parents to raise and instruct children in the Lord's law.

The matter of raising children falls primarily on the mother. This is natural, since no one is so close to the soul and heart of the child as its mother. It is not without reason that a child runs directly to its mother, crying "Mama" when it is hurt. There is a great task before the mother: to raise a son or daughter as a believing Christian, good, responsive, work-loving, useful to the Church and to society, and to raise the child thus by word and example and love and strictness. This is the sanctuary of her service to the Lord; her work is no less important than the husband's work for the family. Shame and dishonor to those mothers who shirk from the raising of their children and give them over to be cared for by hired persons, forgetting that it is so easy to ruin or soil the child's soul. Moreover, can anyone really replace a child's mother?

But children must understand their responsibilities no less than the parents. Everyone knows the fifth commandment of God's law, about honoring the parents. The apostle Paul enjoins children to "obey your parents in the Lord, for this is right" (Eph 6:1). And, of course, this requirement is brought forth precisely by justice. For children are obligated in all things to their parents who take care of them, loving, toiling, denying themselves in much, raising their children by their own love, often helping them even when they have already become adults and independent people.

How often, though, is the fifth commandment violated among us! Even those children who are convinced that they sincerely and deeply love their parents often do not heed them, which means that they do not honor them. Love is always united with obedience. And the older the children become, the more self-willed they become, alas, affronting their parents, reproaching them to their face for their "backwardness" and not considering their authority in anything. Is this respect for parents? In the Old Testament it was plainly stated: "Whatever man curses his father or mother, shall surely be put to death" (Lev 20:9), and in the Gospel the Saviour, reminding us of this law, calls it a commandment of God. How many known incidents there are in life, awful examples of how the Lord severely punished (sometimes even to death) those who offended their father or mother! Not without reason it said that "the prayers of a mother save from water and fire," and "the blessing of parents establishes the home of children." On the other hand, who does not know of the awful misfortune caused by incurring one's father's or mother's curse?

Thus, in its basic sense, the fifth commandment speaks of honoring parents. Nevertheless, it also speaks in consideration of all those who occupy similar positions for a Christian: teachers, educators, etc., and especially, the representatives of lawful authority who preserve the order of society. The apostle Paul directed us to pray "for kings and all who are in authority" (1 Tim 2:2), and in many places in his epistles, he taught to submit to the authorities. More important, of course, for the Christian, is the honoring of Church authorities—the pastors of the Church, especially the bishops, and also the pastor who is his spiritual father and answers before God for his soul. The apostle Paul says, "Obey those who rule over you, be submissive, for they watch out for your souls, as those who must give account" (Heb 13:17). And the Lord Himself said to His Apostles, and in their persons to the pastors of the Church: "He who hears you hears Me, he who rejects you rejects Me, and he who rejects Me rejects Him who sent Me" (Luke 10:16).

POINTS OF REFLECTION

1. Why is being a Christian much more than a choice of one lifestyle among many?

2. What is a Christian marriage?

3. What are the obligations of parents to each other and to their children and of children to their parents?

CHAPTER 23

Family and Society; Patriotism

A strong and healthy family is the first and basic unit of society and of the state. The strongest and most well-organized state will come to a condition of decline and disintegration if its family unit falls apart and there are no bases of family life and upbringing. If, on the other hand, the family unit is strong and the upbringing is healthy, then in the event of a major external destruction of the forms of government and society, the people remain capable of carrying on life and can reestablish the strength and unity of the state.

A Christian family must not lock itself up within itself or turn itself into a "chicken coop." Such a life is family egoism. A person who lives in it has no interests outside his own family, does not want to know of the joys and sorrows of the surrounding world, and does not serve it in anyway. Such a life is not a Christian life and such a family is not a Christian family. A Christian family, as a cell or unit of society, is a part of it and is inseparably united with its whole. It actively participates in the society's life and serves its neighbors.

According to the clear teaching of the Gospel, moreover, the living relationship of the Christian must not be locked up within the framework of the family but must be expressed also in the framework of the national state. Christian love is panhuman. For a Christian, every person is his neighbor whom he must love according to the commandment of the Saviour, regardless of what nation the person might belong to. We are clearly told this by the parable of the merciful Samaritan and especially by its categorical conclusion. In this parable, the Saviour showed the Pharisee the degree of mercy and love, which the good Samaritan bestowed upon the robbed and wounded Jew—a man from a nation inimical to his own. Furthermore, He told the Pharisee, "Go and do likewise" (Luke 10:37). Such is the law of Christian love.

But if we Christians are called to such an all-embracing love, then are we not compelled to accept cosmopolitanism—that teaching of the brotherhood of all people, according to which man is a "citizen of the universe," and not of his own state? According to this teaching, mankind must become one family, without any state or national differences and divisions.

We do not doubt that the positive part of cosmopolitanism's teaching is close to Christianity. It undoubtedly took its appeals for brotherhood, love, and mutual help directly from Christianity. These appeals are purely Christian. It is, however, only these Christian ideas that are of value in cosmopolitanism. Cosmopolitanism has, however, added much distorted falsehood and error to this element of truth. Because of this, its teaching has become narrowly one-sided and artificial and thus not vital. Such errors include all the tenets of cosmopolitanism, which speak against feelings of patriotism and the duty of service to one's native land, its good estate, and safety.

One can, in fact, observe that the lives of the verbose preachers of cosmopolitanism are dry and incapable of sincere, compassionate relationships. While foaming at the mouth they cry about their love for mankind but cannot love their neighbor as is necessary. Christianity does not teach this false, one-sided cosmopolitanism. Christ commanded us to have not an artificial "love for mankind," but real love for neighbor. For a Christian, such a neighbor is each and every person (therefore, a Christian must love everyone), and in particular, each person with whom he meets in daily life. Christian life is manifested most of all in precisely these personal encounters, in living mutual intercourse, mutual support and compassion. It is distant from the one-sided teaching of cosmopolitanism with its appeals for an artificial "love for mankind"; a love which is removed from the realities of life.

As a child, a person's neighbors are his parents, brothers, sisters, and other relatives. At this time, it is sufficient if one is a good, loving, responsive, and dedicated member of the family. The child does not yet have vital relationships with those outside the family. Gradually growing up through childhood and adolescent years, one develops personal, vital relationships with many other people and they become "one's own." Good upbringing must teach the child to treat these new "neighbors" in a Christian manner—to be friendly, of goodwill, to have a sincere readiness to help, and to render as much service as possible. As a person matures, his horizons expand and every human being becomes one's "neighbor," regardless of what nation or race they may belong.

Naturally, one will love one's own family and the relatives he grew up with, most of all, and secondly, the whole country, the people to which one belongs. One is tied to this people both by state and civil obligations and by culture and customs. One is bound to one's people, to one's own homeland, and one loves them. This love for homeland is that Christian patriotism, which cosmopolitanists so strongly struggle against.

Christian patriotism is, of course, alien to those extremes and errors into which "super-patriots" fall. A Christian patriot, while loving his nation, does not close his eyes to its inadequacies but soberly looks at its properties and characteristics. He will never agree with those "patriots" who are inclined to elevate and justify everything native (even national vices and inadequacies). Such "patriots" do not realize that this is not patriotism at all, but puffed-up national pride—that very sin against which Christianity struggles so strongly. No, a true patriot does not close his eyes to the sins and ills of his people; he sees them, grieves over them, struggles with them, and repents before God and other peoples for himself and his nation. In addition, Christian patriotism is completely alien to hatred of other peoples. If I love my own people, then surely I must also love the Chinese, the Turks, or any other people. Not to love them would be non-Christian. No, God grant them well-being and every success, for we are all people, children of one God.

The most important information, which we find concerning patriotism, is in the Holy Scripture. In the Old Testament, all the history of the Jewish people is filled with testimony of how the Jews loved their Sion, their Jerusalem, their temple. This was a model of true patriotism, of love for one's people and its sacred things. Significantly, our Christian Church has adopted this glorification of holy things by the Jews for our own services (although with a slightly different Christian understanding) and chants, "Blessed is the Lord out of Zion, who dwelleth at Jerusalem." Alleluia (Ps 134:21). The prophet Moses showed an especially striking example of love for his people. On one occasion, immediately after having received the testament from God, the Israelite people betrayed their God and worshipped a golden calf. Then, the justice of God's Truth became strongly inflamed. Moses began to pray for his people who had sinned. He remained on the mountain for forty days and forty nights in prayer. The Lord told him, "Now therefore, let Me be, that I may burn in wrath against them and consume them" (Exod 32:9 LXX). In these words of God, there is a remarkable testimony about the power of the prayer of a righteous person, by which he, in the bold words of St John Chrysostom, in some way binds God. The great prophet began to pray even more fervently and finally exclaimed, "Yet now if You will forgive their sin, forgive it—but if not, blot me out of the book You have written" (Exod 32:32). And the Lord hearkened to Moses. Is this not the highest struggle of self-denying patriotism?

We see a similar example in the New Testament in the life of the great apostle Paul. No one hindered his work of preaching more wrathfully and stubbornly than did his fellow countrymen. They hated Paul and considered him to be a betrayer of the faith of their fathers. Nevertheless, the apostle says, "For I could wish that I myself were accursed from Christ for my brethren, my countrymen according to the flesh" (Rom 9:3). From these words, we

see his love for his native people. This love was so great
that, like Moses, he was prepared to sacrifice even his personal, eternal salvation for the salvation of his people.

We have an example in the life of the Saviour Himself. In the Gospel we read that He came only to His own
people and spoke to them first of all. On another occasion,
He said, turning to Jerusalem, "O Jerusalem, Jerusalem,
the one who kills the prophets and stones those who are
sent to her! How often I wanted to gather your children
together, as a hen gathers her brood under her wings"
(Luke 13:34). When He rode into Jerusalem to the cries of
"Hossana" when all the people rejoiced, the Saviour wept.
He did not weep for Himself, but for this, His city, and
because of the ruin of those who were now crying to Him,
"Hossana" (Matt 21:9) but in a few days would cry, "Cru-
cify Him" (Mark 15:13). Thus did He love His own people
with a profound and moving love.

The feeling of patriotism, therefore, is not rejected
and condemned by Christianity. It does not condemn,
despite the false views of cosmopolitanists, the righteousness
of the preeminent love for one's neighbors. We already
know the words of the apostle, "But if anyone does
not provide for his own, and especially for those of his
household, he has denied the faith and is worse than an
unbeliever" (1 Tim 5:8). Once more we emphasize that such
love and care must not be an egoistic, self-enclosing love.

While caring for those with whom one comes into a direct contact, a Christian must never forget other people in his Christian love—his neighbors and brothers in Christ. In conclusion, let us cite these words of the apostle Paul: "Therefore, as we have opportunity, let us do good to all, especially to those who are of the household of faith" (Gal 6:10).

POINTS OF REFLECTION

1. How should the love nurtured within the confines of a family unit reach out beyond itself?

2. Why is patriotism or love of one's homeland a manifestation of Christian love? How does nationalism differ from this?

3. Can Christian love for all be expressed in a way that does not involve concrete persons?

CHAPTER 24

Christian Service; War

Naturally, this Christian patriotism we have spoken of requires from each of us as great a service as possible to the nation. This service is fulfilled most of all in service to the government or society. The value of such service is even more significant if it is rendered unselfishly—free of any material calculations and considerations. A person serves the country in one way or another when he participates in its life, for example, by expressing himself in the press or in civil elections, etc. In this, one must strive to bring benefit to the whole country, the whole people, and not merely to one's own personal or party interests. Then one's conscience will be at peace. It may be that one will not attain great external success, but let him, nevertheless, fulfill the duty of a patriot and a faithful child of the nation in an honorable and Christian manner.

There is a saying, "A friend in need is a friend indeed." Love for the nation is most clearly manifested in times of national trials and troubles. We all know how it feels when someone close to us is ill. We do not want diversions or comforts. In our sorrow and concern, we sometimes cannot even eat or drink or sleep. One who truly loves his nation will manifest similar feelings during times of national troubles. If our heart is filled with nothing but our own personal experiences and interests, if we moan and sigh while our deeds remain far from our words, then our love for the nation is poor indeed.

One of the clearest and most self-denying struggles of service to one's homeland is to die for the nation. A Christian soldier is a defender of the homeland and clearly fulfills Christ's precept, "Greater love has no man than this, than to lay down one's life for his friends" (John 15:13).

War in itself is absolutely evil, an extremely sad phenomenon and deeply contrary to the very essence of Christianity. Words cannot express how joyous it would be if people ceased to war with one another and peace reigned on earth. Sad reality speaks quite otherwise, however. Only some dreamers far removed from reality and some narrowly one-sided sectarians can pretend that war can be omitted from real life.

It is quite correct to point out that war is a violation of the commandment, "Thou shalt not murder" (Exod 20:13). No one will argue against that. Still, we see from the Holy Scriptures that in that very same Old Testament time when this commandment was given, the Israelite people fought on command from God and defeated their enemies with God's help. Consequently, the meaning of the commandment, "Thou shalt not murder" (Exod 20:13), does not refer unconditionally to every act of removing a person's life. This commandment forbids killing for revenge, in anger, by personal decision or act of will. When our Saviour explained the deep meaning of this commandment, He pointed out that it forbids not only actual murder, but also unchristian, vain anger.

Nevertheless, in a conversation with the Apostles about the last days, the Lord told them, "You will hear of wars and rumors of wars. See that you are not troubled; for all these things must come to pass" (Matt 24:6). With these words, the Lord refutes all statements that war is avoidable.

True, we have already examined the fact that war is a negative phenomenon. Yet it will exist, sometimes as the sole defense of truth and human rights, or against seizure, brutal invasion, and violence. Only such wars of defense are recognized in Christian teaching. In fact, we hear of the following event in the life of St Athanasius of the Holy Mountain. Prince Tornikian of Georgia, an eminent commander of the Byzantine armies, was received into monasticism at St Athanasius' monastery. During the time of the Persian invasion, Empress Zoe recalled Tornikian to command the armies. Tornikian flatly refused on the grounds that he was a monk. But St Athanasius said to him,

> We are all children of our homeland and we are obligated to defend it. Our obligation is to guard the homeland from enemies by prayers. Nevertheless, if God deems it expedient to use both our hands and our heart for the common weal, we must submit completely ... If you do not obey the ruler, you will have to answer for the blood of your compatriots whom you did not wish to save, and for the destruction of the churches of God.

Tornikian submitted, defeated the enemy, and rescued the homeland from danger.

In a conversation with Mohammedans, about war, St Cyril, the Enlightener of the Slavs, said, "We meekly endure personal offenses; but as a society, we defend each other, laying down our lives for our neighbors, so that you having taken them captive, do not force them to deny their faith or perform acts against God." Finally, what Russian does not know the example of St Sergius of Radonezh, who blessed Prince Dimitry Donskoy to go to war, prayed for the success of the Russian army, and commemorated those soldiers who died on the field of battle?

One can, of course, sin and sin greatly while participating in war. This happens when one participates in war with a feeling of personal hatred, vengeance, or vainglory and with proud personal aims. On the contrary, the less he thinks about himself, and the more he is ready to lay down his life for others, the closer the Christian soldier approaches the martyr's crown.

POINTS OF REFLECTION

1. What are some of the ways we can render service to the society in which we live and to its government?

2. In what circumstances will the Church bless us to engage in a war? Why is this not inherently sinful?

∾ CHAPTER 25

The Unity of Love for God and for Neighbor

Ascending from our most simple obligations to our highest, we rise to their apex—our obligations in relationship to God.

According to the clear, precise directions of the Holy Scriptures, our main obligation to God is to love Him. This commandment was expressed in the Old Testament with the words, "You shall love the Lord your God with all your heart, with all your soul, and with all your mind. This is the first and great commandment" (Matt 22:37–38).

To this commandment of God's law, our Saviour bound a second: love for neighbor. He said of this commandment that "it is like it: 'You shall love your neighbor as yourself'" (Matt 22:39); that is, it is like the first commandment—love for neighbor is like love for God. The Holy Church, being founded on the words of the Lord,

118

has always set forth the following order in the moral obligations of man: lowest of all are the obligations to oneself. Therefore, love for oneself must be sacrificed in the name of love for God and neighbor. Love for one's neighbor takes precedence over love for oneself, but it is subject to the highest love: love for God Whom we must love most of all.

There is a contemporary theory that great love for God hinders one's love for neighbors. The proponents of this theory claim that man must make the relationship with neighbors his primary concern. By this, they claim, one fulfills one's obligation of love for God. People who advocate this theory are usually set against the struggles of the anchoritic (monastic solitary) life. From their point of view, the anchorite's mode of life is a manifestation of egoism and dislike for others. In their opinion, the anchorite is a person who is occupied exclusively with himself and the salvation of his own soul, and does not think about others at all.

No one will dispute the fact that in serving one's neighbors, a Christian serves God. More than that, love for neighbor is the proof of love for God, as the beloved apostle says, "If someone says, 'I love God,' and hates his brother, he is a liar; for he who does not love his brother whom he has seen, how can he love God whom he has not seen?" (1 Jn 4:20). In serving our neighbors, we serve God, for we fulfill His law of love.

Nevertheless, it is even more certain that our love for God can never hinder our love for neighbors. "God is love" (1 Jn 4:16). By loving God, we lift ourselves up to a higher spiritual atmosphere, an atmosphere of love and a new "inspiration of life." The heart of an Orthodox Christian is filled with such divine love and radiates it everywhere and upon everyone. Thus, contrary to the opinion cited above, love for God does not obstruct love for neighbors, but on the contrary, strengthens and deepens it.

An excellent clarification of this bond between love for God and neighbor is given by one of the great Orthodox ascetics, Abba Dorotheus. He gave the illustration that mankind is like the rim of a wheel. God is the hub, and each person is like a spoke. If we look at a wheel, we notice that the closer the spokes come to the hub, the closer they come to one another. But man can come close to God and neighbor only through love. It is clear that if one loves God, one will inevitably love one's neighbors.

In the history of Orthodox asceticism, we repeatedly see how strugglers, inflamed with love for God, left the world with its temptations. They did this according to the instructions of the apostle of love, John the Theologian, who said, "Do not love the world or the things in the world. If anyone loves the world, the love of the Father is not in him" (1 Jn 2:15). It is wrong to think that the ascetics renounced their love for people in the world. Not at all. They themselves constantly pointed out that they departed not from people, but from the sins, which abound in the world, from the temptations of a sinful, worldly life. They love their brethren in this world incomparably more than those who have remained in this world and participated in its sins. It should not be forgotten that the solitude of these strugglers has always been filled with prayer, and Christian prayer is not merely for oneself, but also for others. History records for us the following incident in the life of St Pachomius the Great, a native of Alexandria. Once, while living in the desert, he learned that the city of Alexandria was being ravaged by famine and epidemic. He spent several days in tears, not even eating the meager ration of food that he allowed himself. His novices begged him to eat and restore his strength, but St Pachomius replied, "How can I eat when my brethren do not have bread?" How far are even the best of us from such love and commiseration?

Such love for God is not only the summit of a Christian's moral ascent, but it is also the basis of his spiritual existence. Without love there cannot be any spiritual life, struggle, or virtue.

The highest service of Christian love is the pastor's service, and it can be fulfilled only by one who can love Christ. This is the reason that our Saviour Himself, in calling apostle Peter to pastorship, asked him, "Simon, son of Jonah, do you love Me more than these?" (John 21:15). Orthodoxy is a religion of love. "By this all men will know that you are My disciples, if you have love for one another" (John 13:35), said the Lord. Here, His words are about the mutual Christian love of people for one another, and also about filial love, and child-like devotion to Him Whom the Gospel constantly calls, "Our Heavenly Father" (see Matt 5:16, 48; 6:1, 8; Mark 11:25–26; Luke 10:21; 11:2). Therefore, the basis of a truly Christian life is a heart that believes in God and is devoted to Him in a child-like manner and is penetrated by a sincere longing for Him, as to the loving and beloved Father.

POINTS OF REFLECTION

1. Can our obedience to the commandment to love God make us less than fully able to also obey the second commandment to love our neighbor?

2. What is the foundation of a truly Christian life?

CHAPTER 26

The Christian Obligation to Know God

If our first and basic obligation to God is to love Him, then it follows naturally that we must know Him. Man will not and cannot love one whom he does not know.

We must observe that the necessity to know God is one of the least fulfilled of our obligations. How different it was in former times when interest in theological matters and religious knowledge was deeply felt by Orthodox souls. St Gregory the Theologian testifies that in his time even merchants in the marketplace turned from their business affairs to discuss the consubstantiality of the Son of God.

Now, many intelligent people, sometimes even those who write and speak on various purely Christian themes, positively fear all theology. They tend to consider all its explanations and questions as somehow remote from life.

Because of this, an oppressive religious ignorance has appeared—a lack of acquaintance with the basic truths of the faith. Take, for example, the masses of intelligent, educated Russian people. They will enumerate for you, without error, all the tsars of the house of Romanov, the main Russian writers, etc. It is considered a disgrace for an educated person not to know this. Ask them, however, the main dogmas of the Christian faith, or to name the twelve Apostles of Christ (people who did immeasurably more for mankind than any tsar or writer) and in nine of ten cases, the result will be lamentable. Even worse is the fact that no one considers this ignorance to be a disgrace, and people even admit it lightheartedly.

It is absolutely necessary that each Orthodox Christian have a knowledge of the content of his faith and its basic truths: the dogma of the Trinity, Divine Love, the Incarnation, the saving death and Resurrection of the Saviour, and the future destiny of the world and of mankind, etc. These questions are not something distant and insignificant; rather they are vital and important to us, for the whole meaning of life hangs upon their answers.

All these questions coalesce into one: is there a God and Who is He? These are questions of singular importance even for people who barely believe. For truly believing people, to know about God is to know what He means to us and what His will is concerning all of us. This is the basic, most important and precious knowledge in life. In fact, Orthodox life itself is defined first of all by the knowledge of God. The Lord Himself, while praying to His Father, said: "And this is eternal life, that they may know You, the only true God, and Jesus Christ whom You have sent" (John 17:3).

From all this, we see that the knowledge of God is our direct Christian duty, and the way to it, in addition to the study of theology, is the contemplation of God. Contemplation of God is the spiritual disposition in which man intentionally introduces into and maintains in his consciousness the thought of God, His highest properties, the matter of our salvation and of our eternal future, etc. Such contemplation of God is especially loved by our Orthodox ascetics, but unfortunately it is not even familiar to most of us.

The knowledge of God is not, however, the mere rational acceptance and remembrance of our Orthodox Christian teaching about faith and life. Christianity is an animated life, an experience of the human heart, and therefore it is not accepted by all people in the same way. The more a person has experienced the truths and commandments of his faith in his personal life, in the inner experience of inner struggle and striving to live according to Christ's Gospel, the deeper does he assimilate Christianity. Conversely, if a person treats his faith dryly, with external formalism, and is not guided by the appeals of Christ's Gospel in his personal life, he will not accept

Christianity into his soul and heart, and the profound content of the truths of Christ's faith will remain alien to him.

POINTS OF REFLECTION

1. What is the relationship between our love for God and our ability to discourse in theology?

2. Can we love God if we know little about Him?

3. Does knowledge involve more than accumulation of information?

CHAPTER 27
The Necessity of Prayer

The knowledge of God is obviously based on faith. This faith is the first response of the human heart to the content of religious truths, an agreement with and acceptance of them. As it strengthens and becomes deeper, this faith eventually brings one's heart to peace in God, to a Christian hope in God. On the other hand, Orthodoxy teaches us that the Christian faith is inseparably bound to love for God. And love always demands a living, personal relationship with the one we love. In our relationship with God, this love is first of all made manifest in prayer.

One who does not pray is not a Christian. Prayer is the first and most essential element in our spiritual life. It is the breath of our soul, and without it, the soul dies, just as the body dies without air. All the vital functions of the body depend upon its breathing. In exactly the same way, one's spiritual life depends on prayer, and a person who does not pray to God is spiritually dead.

Prayer is the conversation of man with God. One who remembers, knows, and loves God will unfailingly turn to Him in prayer. There is a seriously erroneous view of prayer now becoming widespread (especially among young people). People often say, "One must not force oneself to pray. If I desire to pray, I will pray; if there is no desire, there is no need to pray."

This is a complete lack of understanding of the matter. What would one accomplish in one's worldly activity if one did not force oneself to anything, but only did what was desired? Even more so in spiritual life, where everything that is precious and meaningful is acquired by force, by the struggle of work on oneself. Let us again recall that, according to our Saviour, the Kingdom of God (and everything pertaining to it) is attained by force. So it is indispensable for a Christian to firmly accept in his heart that he must pray, no matter what, regardless of his desire or lack of desire. If you have a good desire to pray, thank God from Whom everything good comes, and do not lose the chance to pray from the soul. If you do not have this desire, and the time for prayer arrives, then it is necessary to force yourself, encouraging your lethargic and lazy spirit by reminding it that prayer (like every good deed) is all the more precious in God's eyes when it is given with difficulty. The Lord does not disdain any prayer if one prays sincerely, as best he knows how, even though he has not developed the habit of praying fully and with unfading fervor.

One who lives even a partial spiritual Christian life will always find something about which to pray to Him, because for such a person, God is a loving Father, a Mighty Protector, and an unending Spring of help and strength. The Christian hurries to Him in need and in woe, as a child to its parent. We must only acknowledge our infirmity and weakness and completely "commit ourselves and one another, and all our life unto Christ our God," for in Him is our faith, hope, and love.

In His conversation with the Samaritan woman, our Lord declared that "true worshippers will worship the Father in spirit and in truth" (John 4:23). This is the basic principle of Christian prayer. It must be fulfilled in spirit and truth, and in praying, a Christian must gather all his spiritual powers into one deep, concentrated effort within himself, in his soul, and contemplate the words of the prayer. Obviously, when one has such a correct view of prayer one understands that it is impossible to give the name "prayer" to the act of merely being present at prayer or reading it with the tongue while one's thoughts are far from it. St John Chrysostom says of such "prayers": "Your body is inside the church, but your thoughts have flown to who knows where. The lips pronounce prayers, but the mind counts income, crops, real estate and friends … You do not hear your own prayers—how do you expect that God will hear them?" A Christian must not pray in such a manner. He prays in "spirit and truth" (John 4:24).

He prays in spirit, concentrated in the depth of his "I" through profound experiences of the heart. He prays in truth—not hypocritically, but in a sincere frame of mind, in true supplication to the Incarnate Truth—to Christ the Saviour.

Of course, this does not (in spite of Protestant error) abrogate the necessity of external prayer but only requires its union with internal prayer. Man is not an angel; his soul does not live without the body just as the body does not live without the soul. The apostle Paul says, "Glorify God in your body and in your spirit, which are God's" (1 Cor 6:20). Therefore, the most basic and complete view of prayer is that in which both the internal and external are present. They tightly unite with each other: both inner experience—man's supplication to God, and outer activity—prostrations, standing at prayer, crossing oneself and various actions in the Divine Services.

Ordinarily, there are three distinctive types of prayer: petitioning, glorifying, and thanksgiving. In our prayer books and Divine Services, all these three types are utilized, mutually complementing one another.

A person who prays to God must remember that prayer cannot go unheard if it is sincere and breathes of living faith. The Lord Himself said, "All things are possible to him who believes" (Mark 9:23). The apostle James, also, explains how destructive is doubt in prayer, saying that "he who doubts is like a wave of the sea driven and tossed by the wind" (James 1:6). Such a person should not expect to receive anything from the Lord. In the Holy Gospel, moreover, we often read how the Lord, in healing those who came to Him, told them, "According to your faith let it be to you" (Matt 9:29); "your faith hath made you well" (Matt 9:22). But firmly believing in God's strength, mercy, and help, a Christian must not forget that every petition for his desires must submit to the all-good will of the Heavenly Father, Who knows what we need. In such a state of faith and dedication to God's will, one will thank God equally whether or not the Lord fulfills one's request. This is quite natural, since such a person believes absolutely that God's wisdom and love direct everything to the benefit and good of man. With good reason, we sing this troparion at the funeral service: "O Thou Who by the depth of Thy wisdom dost provide all things out of love for man, and grantest unto all that which is profitable."[2]

POINTS OF REFLECTION

1. What bodily function is prayer analogous to?

2. How should we struggle to pray more?

3. Can we say or hear prayers being read and still not be praying ourselves?

∾ CHAPTER 28
The Model of Christian Prayer

For Orthodox Christians, the model of prayer is, of course, the "Our Father" (the "Lord's prayer"). If we look at its composition and content, we see that externally it is divided into three parts: invocation, seven petitions, and a glorification. In its inner content, it can be divided into three common parts: the main one, which encompasses an invocation and the first three petitions; the petition about daily bread; and three petitions about our personal sins.

What is the foremost thing about which a Christian must pray? About that goal for which we must strive most of all: the Kingdom of God and His Truth. We see that this is the first part of the prayer. In appealing to God as the Heavenly Father, an Orthodox Christian testifies that our true fatherland is not on earth, but in heaven. It is a "building from God, a house not made with hands, eternal in the heavens," the apostle Paul says firmly (2 Cor 5:1).

In this appeal to the Father, a Christian prays that God's name be hallowed, both in the personal life of each of us and in the human history of mankind. It is especially hallowed when we Orthodox Christians, through the example of our own lives, lead unbelievers to glorify the name of our Heavenly Father. Furthermore, we pray that the Kingdom of God be manifested on earth. Observing life, we see in it a constant struggle between two principles: light and darkness, truth and falsehood, good and evil. When we see this, we cannot but pray that there will be a victory of light over darkness and that there will be a triumph of God's Kingdom, the kingdom of Truth and Good.

In the third petition of the Lord's prayer, we pray that God's will be fulfilled in man's life in the same way that it is fulfilled in the Heavenly world. The Christian conscience is aware and firmly convinces us that not only is it our duty, but it is real wisdom and the truth of life to submit to God's will. The Heavenly Father knows what is beneficial and necessary for each one of us and, through His infinite love and goodness, wishes us good and salvation even more than we desire it for ourselves. Therefore, the apostle Peter says, "Cast all your care upon Him, for He cares for you" (1 Pet 5:7).

The fourth petition of the Lord's prayer is the only one that deals with bodily needs. We must ask for ourselves our daily bread, that is, for all that is necessary for bodily life. But what is more than this—"if it is given, thank God, if it is not given—do not be concerned about it" (from a catechism). Of course, by "daily bread" is understood everything essential for us: food, clothing, shelter, and so forth. This fourth petition demonstrates to man that our earthly life with its "worldly cares" is also an object of concern for our Heavenly Father. The apostle Paul says, "Let your conduct be without covetousness; be content with such things as you have. For He Himself has said, 'I will never leave you, nor forsake you'" (Heb 13:5).

The fifth petition of the Lord's prayer concerns forgiveness of sins. In this petition, as elsewhere in His teaching, our Saviour makes it clear that an indispensable precondition of our receiving forgiveness of sins from God is our own forgiveness of our neighbors. But how often this petition is spoken falsely to God? We read, "Forgive us our debts, as we forgive our debtors" (Matt 6:12), while in reality, we neither forgive nor forget but are offended and conceal vexation in our heart, even a desire for revenge. Therefore, each time a Christian repeats this petition, he must consider whether he has forgiven his enemies and offenders. If not, how can he expect forgiveness from God for himself?

The two last petitions, the sixth and seventh ones, speak of one thing: the causes of sin. At first we ask that the seeds of sin be removed from us, that is, that we be delivered from enticements and temptations and then that we be delivered from the evil one, that is, from the root of all sins, Satan. People usually fear external misfortunes: failures, illnesses, poverty, etc. Christianity teaches us to be more fearful for our immortal soul. "Do not fear not those who kill the body but cannot kill the soul. But rather fear Him who is able to destroy both body and soul in hell" (Matt 10:28). Concerning external misfortunes, particularly trials and persecutions endured for the faith, our Lord said to those who suffer them, "Rejoice and be exceedingly glad, for great is your reward in heaven" (Matt 5:12).

It is not external misfortunes and poverty that the Orthodox Christian must fear, but rather he must fear his own sins and falls. Everyone knows how much we become accustomed to sinning, literally sinning at each step and at each moment of our life. Sin is a violation of the Truth of God's Law, and the result of sin is suffering and grief. The Lord's prayer instills in our hearts a great aversion to these spiritual evils so that, while humbly confessing our weakness and inclination toward sin, we ask God to preserve us from falling into sins and to deliver us from the evil master of sin—the devil.

At the end of these seven petitions, there has been added a solemn glorification of God's power, authority, and glory.

This glorification of God's grandeur contains a filial expression of unwavering and clear conviction that everything we ask for will be given to us from the love of the Heavenly Father: for His is the kingdom, the power, and the glory, unto the ages of ages. Amen.

The Lord's prayer is not the only prayer of glorification, however. There are prayers that are purely and simply glorifications (such as "Praise ye the name of the Lord" or "Holy, Holy, Holy ... "). We do not use them as often, but they are representative of the endings of our prayers, especially in the Divine Services. Prayers of glorification must be seen as especially elevated, for in them, we express Christian love for God and bow before the Most High.

The third aspect of prayer is thanksgiving. Quite understandably, a Christian who loves God and knows of His love, mercy, and benefits cannot but experience feelings of thanksgiving in his heart. The most important prayer of thanksgiving is the paramount Divine Service, the Divine Liturgy. Its main part, referred to as the "Thanksgiving or Eucharistic Canon," begins with the words, "Let us give thanks unto the Lord." And the pure, bloodless sacrifice, the sacrifice of truth, the sacrifice of the Body and Blood of Christ, which is given to us in the Mystery of Holy Communion, although it is visibly offered by people, it is invisibly performed by Christ Himself, by His

Grace and all-mighty power, and it is only received by us, with a devotion of thankful love. This is why in the most important moment of the Liturgy, the priest solemnly exclaims, "Thine Own of Thine Own, we offer unto Thee in behalf of all, and for all," while the faithful respond with the hymn of thanksgiving, "We praise Thee, we bless Thee, we give thanks unto Thee, O Lord."[3]

POINTS OF REFLECTION

1. How does the "Our Father" provide a model for all our prayer?

2. Where do we find prayer of thanksgiving most clearly manifested in our liturgical services?

Prayer; Feasts and Fasts

We have discussed how important prayer is for the spiritual life of an Orthodox Christian. But how are we to pray? Two forms of prayer are distinguished in the Orthodox Christian life: private prayer or prayer at home, and communal Church prayer. Each has certain special characteristics. Our Saviour gave instructions in the Gospel about private prayer: "But you, when you pray, go into your room, and when you have shut your door, pray to your Father who is in the secret place; and your Father who sees in secret will reward you openly" (Matt 6:6). And of course, private home prayers must be basic and elementary for us. Prayer is deeply intimate and heartfelt. Everyone who has sincerely searched for heartfelt and moving prayer knows well how easy and natural it is to pray in solitude, in silence, and in peace. Moreover, our Lord firmly warns us against hypocritical prayer done for show, to elicit praise from people.

When a Christian prays to God, he must strive to contemplate the words of the prayers that he reads and to concentrate his thought on the content of the prayers. Everyone knows how difficult it is to struggle against the pressure of outside thoughts and images that tiresomely besiege the praying person. This comes to us both from our personal distraction and from indirect action of the evil, diabolic powers. The task of a Christian is to apply all his powers to persistently shake off all these extraneous thoughts (which are sometimes impure) that torment him and to pray with concentration and piety. One should remember that a powerful onslaught of thoughts and images, primarily vile or blasphemous, comes to us directly from Satan, and the struggle of resisting these thoughts is a direct struggle against evil. Consequently, one receives great benefit from such a struggle, not harm.

Usually, we pray with church prayers, which we learn from childhood. This is necessary, because they lead us into that prayerful atmosphere by which the Church breathes. In this, one must beware not to slide into an automatic, mechanical reading of prayers without attention and penetration into the sense and meaning of the words of the prayer. To this end, full reverence and concentration of attention are demanded so that one actually prays—converses with God and does not skim through the familiar words with superficial attention.

According to the harmonious testimonies of ascetics of prayer (Bishop Theophan the Recluse, St John of Kronstadt, etc.) in addition to the reading of Church prayers, one ought to add prayer in one's own words, about one's personal needs and the needs of one's own neighbors. Often, a Christian cannot fully express his feelings and trials in the words of the written prayers. In such cases, a living, sincere prayer in his own words is appropriate, together with a confession of one's daily sins, with expressions of one's intent to struggle, with God's help, against one's daily sins. Such a prayer will come from the depth of the human soul.

Only the person who develops in himself penetrating and constant prayer at home can correctly participate in the public prayers in church. This participation is a firm necessity for every Christian. The Lord Himself said, "Where two or three [members of the Church] are gathered together in My name, I am there in the midst of them" (Matt. 18:20).

The Ecumenical Patriarch and great teacher of prayer, St John Chrysostom, says,

> One can, of course, also pray at home: but you cannot pray there as you do in church where so many people are gathered, where a harmonious voice is raised to God. You will not as soon be heard, praying alone to God, as when praying together with your brethren, for here is something greater: oneness of mind, a union of love,

the prayers of the priests. During communal prayer, not only do the people send up their own voices to God, but together with them, the angels and archangels glorify the Master.

Thus, church prayer has a preeminently sacred character and it is given this by the Grace of the Holy Spirit, which, as we know, quickens our spiritual life, cooperating with our personal spiritual efforts.

A priest serves in church; he is not a priest because he receives an ecclesiastical education or has a calling to serve the Church. All this only prepares him for pastoral service. He is a priest only because he was consecrated to it by ordination; through the mystery of priesthood he is numbered among the pastors of the Church. So it is that our church is a consecrated church, with a specially consecrated holy table, and the holy antimins, in which are laid the relics of the saints. According to the word of the Holy Scripture, our church is a house of prayer. The Lord gave us an example of the honor due to God's house when, during His earthly sojourn, He twice cleansed it from all disorder and indecency. At the Divine Services, we repeatedly hear the Holy Church exclaim the petition, "For this holy temple, and for them that with faith, reverence, and fear of God enter herein, let us pray to the Lord."[4] Each of us must enter a church with this disposition, remembering that here one stands before the face of the Lord Himself.

One of the greatest and most painfully evident deficiencies of our contemporary life is our inability to celebrate our feasts in a Christian manner. Our lives are composed in such a way that interests of a purely earthly character predominate in them. Jobs, worry over income, and shallow impressions of the day—all this fills our time and man does not have time to simply think about his soul, its demands, and needs. Our feasts become rays of light in our colorless lives filled with vanity and worldly cares. They teach us that this world is not so empty and impoverished as it sometimes seems to us, for above it, there is a different world giving our soul joy and ineffable peace. Who does not know what joy fills the heart of an Orthodox Christian in the days of the greatest feast, Pascha, the Radiant Resurrection of the Lord?

How often, though, do days of Christian commemoration and festivity turn out to be days of even greater emptiness and senseless idleness. A feast is a special day of God and must be dedicated as fully as possible to prayer and deeds of Christian mercy. In our time though, the feasts are often treated as any other day, and sometimes people even use them for debauchery and drunkenness. Of course, one who devotes feast days to bodily relaxation and entertainment differs in no way from pagans and atheists, for he "celebrates the feast" just as they do. How often do we see that people or even whole clubs (societies) and institutions organize their "balls" and entertainments on the eves of feasts? An outrageous and unchristian custom! In the evening a person "enjoys" himself—often to exhaustion, to excess, and not without sin, and in the morning, when God-fearing people are going to the feast day Liturgy, he rests, sometimes until midday. And where is prayer, the attendance at the Church of God? How does such a person differ from an atheist or a pagan?

Yet more reprehensible is the way many people view the fasts that the Holy Church has given us. We have many fasts: four lengthy ones, the Great Fast, the Sts Peter and Paul fast, and the Dormition and Nativity fasts, and also shorter one-day fasts: Wednesdays and Fridays (weekly), the eves of the Nativity and the Baptism of our Lord, the Beheading of St John the Baptist, the Exaltation of the Precious Cross, and Passion Week (especially Great Friday).

What an amazing and unchristian relationship so many people now have to these fasts. The fasts are violated by people without a qualm of conscience, as if the matter was about some nonsense, having no significance. The Church, on the other hand, takes a very serious view of the matter and excludes from Holy Communion those who refuse to keep the fasts without cause. And St Seraphim of Sarov clearly said, "One who does not observe fasts is not a Christian, no matter what he considers or calls himself." Fasting is absolutely indispensable for man. From the external aspect, it is a struggle of absolute, filial obedience to the Church, whose rules are from the Holy Spirit, and not something to be neglected and scorned. From the inner aspect, fasting is a struggle of restraint and self-limitation. In this lies the great value and sense of fasting, since a strict observance of fasts tempers one's will and perfects the character of one who is firm in his religious convictions and actions. Let us not forget that Christ Himself fasted and foretold that His apostles would also fast. And concerning the battle with evil, diabolic power, He said, "This kind does not go out except by prayer and fasting" (Matt 17:21).

We hear people claiming that fasting is harmful to health. But strict fasting is not demanded of ill people, who fast only according to their strength. Most important, one should remember that only those people who themselves do not fast speak about the "harm" of fasting. But those who do observe fasting will never say this, for they know through personal experience that not only is fasting not harmful, but it is positively beneficial to bodily health.

Fasting is not merely a restraining from food, however. During the days of the fasts, the Church sings, "While fasting bodily, let us also fast spiritually." True fasting includes deeds of Christian mercy. It is an alienation of the evil one, a restraint of the tongue, a laying aside of anger, a cutting off of vices, talkativeness, falsehood, and swearing. Thus, for a Christian, fasting is a time of restraint and self-education in all respects, and a real Christian period of fasting gives believers a great moral satisfaction. The teacher of Christian asceticism, Bishop Theophan the Recluse, says of fasting: "Fasting appears gloomy until one steps into its arena: but begin, and you will see that it is the light after darkness, freedom after bonds, release after a burdensome life."

POINTS OF REFLECTION

1. What are the two forms of prayer and how do they relate to each other?

2. When or where should we use our own words in prayer?

3. What is the importance of celebrating Feast Days to growth in our spiritual life?

4. Why are we always being told to fast for particular days or periods? Is this really essential to living a Christian life?

Metropolitan Philaret of New York

A Short Biography
of Metropolitan Philaret

His Eminence, Metropolitan Philaret, whose secular name was George Nicholaevich Voznesensky, was born in Kursk on March 22, 1903 (O.S.). His mother, Lydia Vasilievna, reposed when he was eighteen, and his father subsequently took the monastic tonsure, receiving the name Dimitry. He was subsequently ordained to the episcopate and was repatriated (from Manchuria) to the USSR, where he reposed in 1947.

In 1909, the family of Metropolitan Philaret moved to Blagoveshchensk, on the Amur River, where young George completed his studies at an eight-grade secondary school. Emigrating with his family to Harbin, Manchuria, he enrolled in the Russo-Chinese Polytechnic Institute and graduated from it in 1927 with a degree in electromechanical engineering. In 1931 he completed pastoral courses in theology at the St. Vladimir Institute in Harbin. Later, he was to serve there as an instructor in New Testament, Pastoral Theology, and Homiletics. Ordained to the diaconate in 1930, in 1931 he received the monastic tonsure with the new name Philaret;

that same year he was ordained to the rank of hieromonk. In 1933 Father Philaret was elevated to the rank of abbot (hegumen) and in 1937 to the rank of archimandrite.

One of Vladyka Philaret's colleagues at the Institute remembers:

> Father Archimandrite Philaret undertook the great, celestial, and pastoral activity of teaching. The faithful would pack the church in which he was serving. All levels of Harbin's Orthodox populace loved him. The name of Archimandrite Philaret was widely known even beyond the boundaries of the Diocese of Harbin. He was kind and accessible to everyone who turned to him; and there were many who did. Going to him, they knew they would receive good advice, that they would find consolation and help. Father Archimandrite Philaret was quite strict with himself; he was well-known as a true ascetic. And what a rare memory our good, kind Vladyka possessed! When we met him, he showed great interest in all aspects of our life: he didn't have to be reminded of our needs or difficulties; he had already developed with us the theme of our conversation, and gave ready answers.

After Manchuria was occupied by the Soviet forces, difficult days began in Harbin. Deceived by false information on the state of the Church in Russia, the aged Metropolitan Melety acknowledged the authority of the Patriarchate of Moscow over himself and his clergy. Among the clergy was Archimandrite Philaret. However, he adamantly refused to accept a Soviet passport. When interviewed by a newspaper reporter who asked how he viewed "the wise step of the Soviet government which is offering the populace of Harbin the opportunity to be reinstated as citizens of their native land," Archimandrite Philaret gave the following bold reply:

> I do not consider it possible to accept, nor will I accept, Soviet citizenship, until such time as I am really convinced, beyond a shadow of a doubt, one hundred percent, that the persecution of religion, antireligious propaganda, and the hunting down of the ministers of the Church has ceased entirely, and the Church, which did not separate, but was driven from the country, has resumed the position befitting it there.

Archimandrite Philaret thus, until the end of his residence in China, refused to accept Soviet citizenship, despite all the danger attendant upon such a position. On another occasion, Archimandrite Philaret was subjected to persecution for his boldness. Having become acquainted with an issue of the *Journal of the Moscow Patriarchate*, in which Lenin's name appeared in a list of titles of foremost benefactors of the human race, Archimandrite Philaret expressed his indignation in a sermon, which became widely known.

His fearless denunciation of the godless Communists incited their particular rage, and they decided to burn Archimandrite Philaret alive, setting fire to his cell. But the Lord preserved His chosen one: although badly burned, he escaped from the fiery trap alive.

Protecting his flock in every way possible, he, as he himself put it, "never defiled [his] lips or his prayer with prayer for the servants of Antichrist," despite repeated threats. Furthermore, over the course of several years, Archimandrite Philaret communicated with Metropolitan Anastassy, the head of the Russian Orthodox Church Abroad, through various channels, despite the danger that this entailed.

The Synod of Bishops long and persistently endeavored to obtain an exit visa for him, and, judging by the correspondence preserved in the archives, nearly every diocese of the Church hoped to obtain him for itself. Only in 1962 was the Synod of Bishops successful in securing the release of Archimandrite Philaret to Hong Kong, from which he departed almost immediately for Brisbane, Australia. A significant number of Father Philaret's former parishioners had settled in Australia, and soon after his arrival there a petition was submitted to the Synod, over many signatures, requesting that Archimandrite Philaret be consecrated bishop for Brisbane.

At the Council of Bishops of 1964, at which Metropolitan Anastassy retired, Bishop Philaret, a vicar bishop who had come to the council with Archbishop Savva, his ruling bishop, was elected First Hierarch. He held that position for twenty-one years.

Nearly midway through his tenure as First Hierarch, the Third Pan-Diaspora Council was convoked in 1974. Especially memorable for our faithful are the four canonizations of saints, which were celebrated within the past twenty years: St John of Kronstadt, St Herman of Alaska, St Xenia the Blessed of Petersburg, and the New Martyrs and Confessors of Russia.

Our First Hierarch repeatedly appealed to the heads of other Churches in admonitory letters, and several hierarchs heeded his voice. Vladyka Metropolitan was an excellent preacher.

A profound faith, ardent prayer, kindness, and benevolence, care that spiritual peace not be violated, and steadfast confession of the Truth were the characteristic traits of our departed First Hierarch, Vladyka Metropolitan Philaret.

The Transfer of the Blessed Remains
of Metropolitan Philaret

To the Cathedral Church of Holy Trinity Monastery, on November 8/21, 1985, on the joyous feast day of the Synaxis of Archangel Michael and All the Heavenly Hosts, the All-merciful Lord sent His angel to receive the pure and bright soul of one of the marvelous strugglers of our century, the Most Reverend Metropolitan Philaret, the third First Hierarch of the Russian Church Abroad. The Lord received a suffering soul, for it is certain that Vladyka suffered greatly in the last days of his earthly life, afflicted by a severe physical illness. However, the Metropolitan suffered spiritually as well over the departure from the Truth of preserved. Archbishop Laurus immediately informed all the members of the Hierarchal Synod of the inspiring discovery.

On Thursday, the eve of the Synaxis of Archangel Michael, at the scheduled time for the transferal of the remains of the Metropolitan, a heavy, warm rain began. Therefore, the planned procession to accompany the remains of Metropolitan Philaret from

the cemetery had to be cancelled, and his remains were brought
to the cathedral by automobile. He also sorrowed for the Russian
Church Abroad, for it was often afflicted by sorrows and persecution. Finally, Metropolitan Philaret sorrowed for the indifferent
people who had become lost and Orthodox only by name, having
cut themselves off from the Church. He would sorrowfully entreat
them saying: "You unfortunate people, you are robbing yourselves,
denying yourselves of the Grace-filled life in the Church."

On the day after the funeral service for Metropolitan Philaret
in the Synodal Cathedral of the Mother of God of the Sign, on
Sunday, November 11/24, 1985 (the day of the discovery of the
Myrrh-Streaming Iveron Icon of the Mother of God), Vladyka
was temporarily buried in the sepulchre below the Dormition
church in the cemetery of Holy Trinity Monastery. I remember
the freezing rain that day; everything was covered with ice.

In 1997 the construction of additional crypts under the altar
of the Holy Trinity Cathedral was completed and the sacristy and
vestry on the north and south sides of the altar were extended.
The remains of Metropolitan Philaret could now be transferred
from the cemetery to a permanent resting place at the Cathedral.
The translation of the remains was scheduled for the thirteenth
anniversary of Vladyka's repose, November 8/21, 1998. Prior
to this, the remains were examined by Archbishop Laurus on
Tuesday, November 4/17, with the help of a few members of the
brotherhood. Despite the fact that the remains lay in a very damp
basement crypt for thirteen years, when the totally undamaged
wooden coffin was opened, it was discovered that the Metropolitan's body had dried, but had not corrupted. His skin had taken on
a bronze color. At three o'clock in the afternoon the cathedral was

full of members of the Brotherhood and pilgrims. On the porch of the church, awaiting the arrival of the relics were the abbot of the monastery, Archbishop Laurus, with a multitude of clergy. Priests carried the coffin on their shoulders into the church. The coffin, covered with the original blue mantle, was placed in the middle of the church. [This same mantle had covered the coffin for thirteen years in the sepulchre without any decomposition.] Four novices stood like guards, two on each side of the coffin, holding fans and dikiri and trikiri. Immediately a very solemn panikhida began, served by Archbishop Laurus with twelve priests and two deacons.

Although intentionally no announcements had been made regarding the transfer of Metropolitan Philaret's remains, a significant number of the Metropolitan's spiritual children and others who venerated his memory were present. Natural and awe-struck emotions hastened the rapid spread of the news that Vladyka's remains were discovered to be incorrupt.

The rest of the day went as usual in the monastery. The Rule for Communion with an Akathist sung to Archangel Michael preceded the festive All Night Vigil, which was served by Archbishop Laurus, accompanied by visiting and local clergy. The monastery choir sang solemnly under the direction of hieromonk Roman. The unusually warm day ended in fog, typical for this hilly region.

On Saturday, November 8/2 in the morning, the first snowflakes of the season appeared, but the sun and wind soon dried the monastery grounds, and a beautiful day began. The meeting of the Archbishop occurred at 8:45 a.m. with eighteen priests and eleven deacons. There were about three hundred faithful in the cathedral. As is typical in the monastery, the Divine Liturgy was served prayerfully and with grandeur, with the participation of the monastic choir. Protopresbyter Valery Lukianov gave a sermon before the Communion of the faithful, speaking about the life of the ever-memorable Hierarch who, in great measure, fulfilled the pledge of true Christian piety through the labor of prayer, fasting, good deeds, and spiritual learnedness. All of his life Vladyka Philaret stood fast guarding the Truth and attained world renown for his "Sorrowful Epistles" addressed to all Orthodox bishops of the world. In these epistles he warned against the dangers of ecumenism. His last words, "Preserve what you have!," directed to his flock in a testament written just a few days before his death, have a deeper and more crucial significance for us today.

Before the panikhida, Archbishop Laurus gave a very warm talk, in which he informed the faithful of the state of Metropolitan Philaret's relics, and explained that the coffin was not open for people to pay their last respects because that had been done already at his funeral. Besides this, Vladyka said that the opening of relics must be approved by a Hierarchal Council, and if the Lord grants this to happen, then this must be done with special and necessary preparations. It is likely that a commission will be established to examine this matter and for the collection of accounts of miraculous help to people through the prayers of the blessed Metropolitan.

After the panikhida it took some time for all the faithful to venerate the coffin. A touching moment followed as six clergymen ordained by Metropolitan Philaret—three priests and three deacons—raised the coffin on their shoulders and began the procession of the remains around the church to their resting place in the northeastern crypt under the altar. A litya was served here and the coffin was lowered into the grave. The grave was not filled; instead only a small amount of soil was poured on top of the coffin.

The weather was fine, cool, and dry. The wind chased the clouds over the picturesque hills; birds, cheered by the fair weather, joyously sang their songs. The faithful, grateful for such a rare and prayerful solemnity, dispersed with a good disposition in their souls, treasuring in their hearts warm memories of a meek and kindly bishop, whom the Lord sent to the Russian Church in difficult times for Orthodox Christians seeking salvation in the Truth. The faithful left this holy place with the desire to follow, as much as possible, the path of spirituality and piety laid out for the children of the Church by its dear Hierarch-ascetic. The faithful were strengthened by their hope for assistance from the heavenly angels whose feast day was celebrated with such prayerfulness and love on that truly Spirit-filled and luminous day.

—Protopresbyter Valery Lukianov

Metropolitan Philaret on Christianity and Communism

Let us now examine the question of the relationship of Christianity with communism—more precisely, to that particular form of communism, which has now appeared as an attempt to realize the ideas of socialism. This form of communism emerged in history as a sworn and bitter enemy of Christianity. For its part, Christianity recognizes it as completely alien to and inimical with itself.

The history of the Church in Apostolic times reveals that, in those times, it had its own Christian communism and the faithful held everything in common, as the Acts of the Apostles says. Even now, this Christian communism exists in the form of cenobitic monasticism. Both the concept and reality of communal property are a bright, idealistically elevated type of Christian interrelationship, examples of which have always existed in the Orthodox Church.

How great is the difference between such Christian communism and Soviet communism? One is as far from the other as the heavens are from the earth. Christian communism is not an independent self-motivated goal to which Christianity might strive. Rather, it is an inheritance bred of that spirit of love by which the Church has breathed from the first. Moreover, Christian communism is totally voluntary. No one says, "Give us what is yours, it belongs to us." Rather, Christians themselves sacrificed; "neither did anyone say that any of the things he possessed was his own, but they had all things in common" (Acts 4:32).

The communalism of property in Soviet communism is a self-motivated goal, which must be attained, no matter what the consequences and regardless of any considerations. The builders of this type of communism are attaining it by purely violent means, not balking at any measure, even the slaughter of all those who do not agree. The foundation of this communism is not freedom, as in Christian communism, but force; not sacrificial love, but envy and hatred.

In its struggle against religion, Soviet communism goes to such excesses that it excludes even that most elementary justice that is recognized by everyone. In its class ideology, Soviet communism tramples on all justice. The object of its work is not the common good of all the citizens of the state, but only the interests of a single class. All the remaining state and social groupings of citizens are "thrown overboard," outside the care and protection of the communist government. The ruling class has no concern for them.

In speaking of its new order, its "free" state, communism constantly promises a "dictatorship of the proletariat." It became clear long ago, however, that there is no sign of this promised dictatorship of the proletariat, but instead, there is a bureaucratic dictatorship over the proletariat. Moreover, there is no manifestation of ordinary political freedom under this system: neither freedom of the press, nor freedom to assemble, nor the inviolability of the home. Only those who have lived in the Soviet Union know the heaviness and intensity of the oppression that reigns there. Over all this, there reigns a political terror such as has never before been experienced: executions and murders, exiles and imprisonment in unbelievably harsh conditions. This is what communism has given to the Russian people instead of the promised freedom.

In its political propaganda, communism claims that it is attaining the realization of freedom, equality (i.e., justice), and brotherhood. We have already spoken of the first and second. The idea of "brotherhood" was borrowed from the Christians who call each other "brother." The apostle Peter said, "Honor all people. Love the brotherhood" (1 Pet 2:17). In practice, communism exchanged the word "brother" for the word "comrade." This is very indicative, since comrades can be co-participants (but not brethren) in any activity. But one cannot really speak of "brotherhood" anyway, where class struggle, envy, and hatred are preached.

All these cited differences between Christianity and communism do not yet exhaust even the very essence of the contradiction between them. The fundamental difference between communism and Christianity lies deeper still, in the religious ideology of both. No wonder, then, that the communists struggle so maliciously and stubbornly against our faith.

Communism is supposedly an atheistic system that renounces all religion. In actual fact, it is a religion—a fanatical, dark, and intolerant religion. Christianity is a religion of heaven; communism, a religion of the earth. Christianity preaches love for everyone; communism preaches class hatred and warfare and is based on egoism. Christianity is a religion of idealism, founded on the faith of the victory of God's truth and love. Communism is a religion of dry, rational pragmatism, pursuing the goal of creating an earthly paradise (a paradise of animalistic satiety and spiritual reprobation). It is significant that, while a cross is put on a Christian's grave, the grave of a communist is marked by a red stake. How indicative and symbolic for both! With the one—faith in the victory of life over death and good over evil. With the other—ignorant darkness, gloom and emptiness, without joy, comfort, or hope for the future. While the sacred relics of the holy ascetics of Christ's faith blossom with incorruptibility and fragrance, the rotting corpse of the often-embalmed Lenin is the best symbol of communism.

Notes

1 Archbishop Averky in his work "The Acts of the Apostles" refers to this text—"Do not do anything that you would not have others do to you also"—as a fifth requirement that "is found only in certain ancient manuscripts and St John Chrysostom does not refer to it in his commentary." Averky (Taushev), *The Acts of the Apostles*. Jordanville, NY; Holy Trinity Publications, 2017, p. 74.

2 *The Order of the Moleben and the Panikhida*. Jordanville, NY: Holy Trinity Publications, 2021, p. 68.

3 *The Divine Liturgy of Our Father among the Saints John Chrysostom*. Jordanville, NY: Holy Trinity Publications, 2015, p. 175.

4 Ibid., p. 73 [*The Divine Liturgy*].

Scripture Index

New Testament

HOLY TRINITY PUBLICATIONS
JORDANVILLE, NEW YORK

PSJP PRINTSHOP OF
SAINT JOB OF POCHAEV

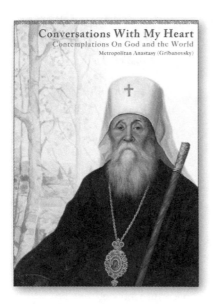

Conversations with My Heart

Contemplations
on God and the World

*By Metropolitan Anastasy
(Gribanovsky)*

Metropolitan Anastasy was the second primate of the Russian Orthodox Church Abroad (1936-1964). These reflections from his diary, which he writes "are part of my very essence," offer the groanings of his heart and his musings on the eternal mercy of God. They draw upon wisdom from sources as diverse as writers of classical antiquity, authors, composers and inventors of the age of enlightenment, offering unique perspectives on these. This volume also contains a short life of the author.

ISBN: 9780884654728

HOLY TRINITY
PUBLICATIONS
JORDANVILLE, NEW YORK

PRINTSHOP OF
SAINT JOB OF POCHAEV

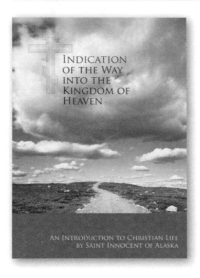

Indication of the Way into the Kingdom of Heaven

An Introduction to Christian Life

By Bishop Innocent (Veniaminov)

People were not created merely to live here on earth like animals that disappear after their death, but to live with God and in God, and to live not for a hundred or a thousand years, but to live eternally.

This book, first published in Aleut in 1833, offers a classic Christian response to questions that we all must address at some point in our life: Why are we here and where can we truly find happiness and prosperity? In a time when the futility of the never-ending pursuit of material gain is being recognised more widely this work is more relevant then ever. It is further enhanced with points for reflection at the end of each section.

ISBN: 9780884653035